To my dear husband Steve
and my three children Sam, Jess and Nick

First published by ABC Books for the
AUSTRALIAN BROADCASTING CORPORATION
GPO Box 9994 Sydney NSW 2001

First published in March 2008

ISBN 978 0 7333 2041 5

Cover by Christa Moffitt, Christabella Designs
Internal layout by Agave Creative Group
Indexing by Jon Jermey @ www.webindexing.biz/
Printed in Hong Kong by Quality Printing

5 4 3 2 1

Contents

Introduction   ix

Prayers and Reflections   1

Glossary   198

Acknowledgements   200

A Note on Sources   202

Index of Contributors   205

Index of Sources   209

About the Author   212

If a man reaches the heart of his own religion,
he has reached the heart of others too.
There is only one God, but there are many paths to him.

Mahatma Gandhi (1869-1948)

Introduction

Mosaic is a collection of favourite prayers and reflections chosen by a broad range of inspirational Australians from a variety of ancestries and faiths. My vision for this book is to offer readers an appreciation of aspirations that are common to everyone, as well as to show a variety of expressions in the quest for purpose in life.

The idea for compiling *Mosaic* had its genesis in the London bombings on 7 July 2005. I was in London at the time, and this tragic event distressed me greatly. It made me feel powerless and vulnerable – especially as one of the suicide bombers lived on the same road as my twin brother – so I was determined to channel my concerns into something constructive and positive. Hence the birth of *Mosaic*.

The concept of a mosaic, where a whole design is composed of a combination of myriad elements, resonates with a vision I hope most Australians share: diverse people of many beliefs, faiths and backgrounds who are able to live peacefully together as one nation. My hope is that *Mosaic* will build bridges and assist in the 'dialogue of living' within Australia's multicultural and spiritually diverse society.

I contacted over 450 people, chosen to represent a cross-section of modern Australia and I received over 165 responses. My passion for meeting new people and engaging with their distinctive spiritual and cultural heritage has made *Mosaic* an exhilarating project to work on. From my research and contacts with many organisations, participants and colleagues, I relished the excitement of an unexpected contribution and found myself passionate about researching the writers' biographies and their reflections.

Mosaic represents a snapshot of life in contemporary Australia, with selected quotations and thoughts from people who range from quiet achievers to high-profile individuals. Many contributors are well-known in their particular field; some have survived severe trauma or shown great resilience in adversity; and others have dedicated their time and energy to building bridges across the divisions in our society.

My sincere thanks go to all the contributors of *Mosaic* and their generosity of spirit in sharing a favourite source of strength. Strong themes that have emerged from the contributions include: a desire for connection with others; the recognition of support from family and friends; the deep sense of comfort given by a familiar prayer; a desire to reinforce the mystery, power and celebration of 'God'; the significance of an individual's identity; the importance of forgiveness; faith in action; the mapping out a sense of purpose in life and the fulfilment of dreams.

I know that *Mosaic* cannot be all things to all people. While I endeavoured to discuss *Mosaic* with as broad a cross-section of people as possible, I realise I have only scratched the surface. Given more time there are many other inspirational Australians from different faiths and backgrounds whom I would like to have included.

The passages in *Mosaic* are arranged in alphabetical order of contributor. The format includes a short biographical note on the contributor followed by their chosen passage and their reflections on their choice. In many cases, these latter words are as powerful as their selected words, making *Mosaic* both unique and personal. The sources of the extracts, along with other relevant information, are given at the end of each contribution. Every effort has been made to source all quotations; however there are instances where this was not possible.

The proceeds I receive from this book will go to two non-profit organisations: The Asylum Seekers Centre of New South Wales, which offers welcome and support for community-based asylum seekers; and Bethlehem Communities Australia, which assists disadvantaged people in the Philippines.

I hope you will find *Mosaic* not only enjoyable and informative, but also as a guiding compass to look beyond your own 'patch' and to engage with others. I hope, too, that these prayers and reflections will encourage a greater depth of contemplation and discovery during those quiet moments.

Rosalind Bradley
www.mosaicbook.com.au

favourite prayers and reflections
from inspiring australians

mosaic

MOHAMAD ABDALLA

Muslim community leader Mohamad Abdalla was born in Libya of Palestinian parents, and grew up in Jordan and Australia. He established the Griffith University Islamic Research Unit in Brisbane, which aims to encourage research into issues that relate to Islam and Muslims in an Australian context.

Verily, God sets forth parables for you, and He directs admonition towards you in order that [your] hearts will be quickened. Surely, the hearts are dead until God quickens them. Justice has signs and portents. As for its signs, they are shyness, generosity, humility, and gentleness. As for its portents, they are embodied in mercy. He has [likewise] made for every affair a gate, and He has made that gate accessible by providing a key. The gate of justice is a deep consideration of consequences, and its key is otherworldliness. Consideration of consequences ultimately involves remembering death, and preparing for it by freely parting from one's wealth. Otherworldliness involves dealing justly with everyone and being satisfied with what suffices. If one is not satisfied with what suffices him, no amount of wealth will ever enrich him.

Umar bin al-Khattab

Reflections

In a time when we are aware of injustices being inflicted on many people in different parts of the world, Umar's advice on what constitutes justice is timely. The act of injustice occurs because of hatred for others or greed – or sometimes a combination of both. A deep 'consideration of consequences' and 'being satisfied with what suffices' are two important qualities which are lacking from many of our world leaders. Cultivating these qualities may hopefully lead to justice.

■ Excerpt from Umar bin al-Khattab, in Salih ibn 'Abdullah ibn Humayd, *Nadr al-Na'im fi Makarim Akhlaq al-Rasul al-Karim*, translated by Zaid Shakir, Jeddah, Saudi Arabia, 2000, vol. 7, p. 2811. Umar bin al-Khattab was the second caliph of Islam.

RANDA ABDEL-FATTAH

A practising lawyer and author, Randa is of Palestinian and Egyptian parentage. Her two novels focus on the difficulties faced by teenage girls growing up as Australian Muslims in contemporary Australia. Randa is also involved with various Palestinian human rights campaigns.

O mankind! We created you from a single (pair) of a male and a female, and made you into nations and tribes, that ye may know each other (not that ye may despise (each other). Verily the most honoured of you in the sight of Allah is (he who is) the most righteous of you. And Allah has full knowledge and is well acquainted (with all things).

Qur'an 49:13

Reflections

This verse has touched me because of its profound wisdom. It is a beautiful reinforcement of God's will that we live with a spirit of egalitarianism and tolerance in this world. I also find it a lovely reinforcement of the equality between men and women.

● Qur'an 49:13, translated by Yusuf Ali, 1934

○○○

AZIZA ABDEL-HALIM, AM

Aziza migrated to Australia from Egypt as a young teacher, wife and mother. Strongly committed to multiculturalism and inter-faith dialogue, Aziza's many positions include president of the Muslim Women's National Network Australia and deputy chair of the Regional Islamic Da'wah Council of South-East Asia and the Pacific Women's Movement.

> Goodness leads to happiness,
> Happiness leads to forgiveness,
> Forgiveness leads to love,
> Love leads to giving,
> Giving leads to receiving,
> Receiving leads to joy,
> Joy leads to appreciation,
> Appreciation leads to understanding,
> Understanding leads to God,
> God, The One and Only!
>
> Abdullah Yusuf Ali

Reflections

This reflection sums up for me the teachings and spirit of Islam: submission to the 'One and Only' God; that faith and action must go together; that selflessness and work to help others is the best way to help humanity, and in helping humanity you are achieving the highest degree of happiness yourself, basking in God's light and pleasure.

Reflection by Abdullah Yusuf Ali, in *How to Live Our Daily Life According to the Teaching of the Qur'an*, Liza Abdullah, Selangor Darul Ehsan Malaysia, 1990.

Abdullah Yusuf Ali (1872–1952) was an Islamic scholar, poet and translator of the Qur'an into English.

○○○

AVRIL ALBA

A scholar of religion since an early age, Avril has a masters degree in comparative religion from Harvard Divinity School. She is director of education at the Sydney Jewish Museum.

If I am not for myself, who will be for me?
And if I am only for myself, what am I?
And if not now, when?

Rabbi Hillel

Reflections

Although deceptively simple, this axiom encapsulates the complex reality in which we all live, work, play and love. As life goes on, it increases in difficulty, and in our desire for simplicity, it is tempting to either subsume the self in the name of 'the greater good' or, alternatively, turn away from the community as a means of control and self-preservation.

What the sages remind us of is that to succumb to either position is to relinquish what it means to truly live: to actively engage with the self and with one's community, and in so doing contribute toward the ongoing mending (in Hebrew, *tikkun*) of the world. However, there is no idealisation of this lifelong project. Rabbi Hillel exemplifies the wisdom of classical Jewish sources and their ability to explore the dialectics of human experience. They require the individual to challenge and care for both self and others as the foundational experiences of a truly spiritual life.

● Rabbi Hillel, *Pirkei Avot* 1:14. *Pirkei Avot*, usually translated as *Ehics of the Fathers*, is a collection of rabbinic sayings found in the Mishnah, the central text of the Jewish Oral Law, codified circa 200–300 CE.

○○○

VIC ALHADEFF

As a journalist, Vic Alhadeff has worked in Russia, Berlin, Israel and South Africa. He is chief executive officer of the New South Wales Jewish Board of Deputies and a former editor of *Australian Jewish News*.

We ask ourselves, 'Who am I to be brilliant, gorgeous, talented, fabulous?' Actually, who are you not to be? You are a child of God. Your playing small doesn't serve the world. There's nothing enlightened about shrinking so that other people won't feel insecure around you. We are all meant to shine, as children do. We were born to make manifest the glory of God that is within us. It's not just in some of us; it's in everyone. And as we let our own light shine, we unconsciously give other people permission to do the same. As we're liberated from our own fear, our presence automatically liberates others.

Marianne Williamson

Reflections

I have long been inspired by this passage. In it, Marianne Williamson – who presents herself as a 'professional positive-thinker' – expands on her idea that our deepest fear is not that we are inadequate but that we are powerful beyond measure.

Intriguingly, her words are customarily attributed to South Africa's national hero, Nelson Mandela. The mysterious, unknown person who incorrectly attributed it to Mandela turned Williamson's inspirational thought into the most famous words she has ever written. 'It's a total urban myth,' she said of the claim that Mandela spoke her words, much less included them in his 1994 inauguration speech as the new president of South Africa – 'I have absolutely no idea how it happened'.

⬤ Selection from p. 191 of *A Return to Love* by Marianne Williamson. Copyright ©1992 Marianne Williamson. Reprinted by permission of HarperCollins Publishers US. Portions reprinted from *A Course in Miracles*. Copyright ©1975 by Foundation for Inner Peace, Inc.
    Marianne Williamson (1952–) is an author and lecturer in spirituality and metaphysics.

DOCTOR
AMEER ALI

Currently a visiting fellow in the Business School at Murdoch University, Ameer is a former president of the Australian Federation of Islamic Councils. He is active in inter-faith dialogue, and chairs the Muslim Community Reference Group, which was formed by the Australian Government in 2005.

Thanks be to my Lord; He the Adorable, and only to be adored. My Lord, the Eternal, the Ever-existing, the Cherisher, the True Sovereign whose mercy and might overshadow the universe; the Regulator of the world, and Light of the creation. He is our worship; to Him belongs all worship; He existed before all things, and will exist after all that is living has ceased. Thou art the adored, my Lord; Thou art the master, the Loving and Forgiving; Thou bestowest power and might on whom Thou pleasest; him whom Thou hast exalted none can lower; and him whom Thou hast lowered none can exalt. Thou, my Lord, art the Eternal, the Creator of all, All-wise, Sovereign, Mighty; Thy knowledge knows everything; Thy beneficence is all-pervading; Thy forgiveness and mercy are all-embracing. O my Lord, Thou art the helper of the afflicted, the Reliever of all distress, the Consoler of the broken-hearted; Thou art present everywhere to help Thy servants, Thou knowest all secrets, all thoughts, art present in every assembly, Fulfiller of all our needs, Bestower of all blessings. Thou art the friend of the poor and bereaved; my Lord, Thou art my Fortress; a Castle for all who seek Thy help. Thou art the Refuge of the weak; the Helper of the pure and true. O my Lord, Thou art my Supporter, my Helper, the Helper of all who seek thy help ... O my Lord, Thou art the Creator, I am only created; thou art my Sovereign, I am only Thy servant; Thou art the helper, I am the beseecher; Thou my Lord art my refuge; Thou art the Forgiver, I am the sinner; Thou my Lord, art the merciful, All-knowing, All-loving;

I am groping in the dark; I seek Thy knowledge and love.
Bestow my Lord, all Thy knowledge and love and mercy;
forgive my sins. O my Lord, and let me approach Thee,
my Lord.

Ameer Ali Syed

Reflections

This prayer comes from Ali ibn Abi Talib, (?600–661 CE), the fourth Caliph of Islam. Soon after the death of the Prophet Muhammad a successor was needed to administer and govern the emerging Muslim community. Abu Baker – the father of Ayesha, the wife of the Prophet, and the most senior and respected of the prophet's companions – was chosen to assume that role. 'Caliph' was the title chosen by Abu Baker. After him Umar and Uthman succeeded as the second and third caliphs respectively. Ali ibn Abi Talib, the son-in-law of the Prophet, became the fourth caliph in the year 656 CE.

This prayer of Ali evinces the highest devotional spirit and it can be said by any individual, irrespective of their religion. This prayer was given to me by my father when I was fifteen years old, and I still recite it.

● Excerpt from Ameer Ali Syed, *The Spirit of Islam: the life and teachings of Muhammad*, Gorgias Press, London, 1949.
Ameer Ali Syed (1849–1928) was a prominent 'liberal' thinker among modern Muslims. He put forward the idea that if Muslims were to have an honoured place in public life, they should organise themselves politically.

MAHSHEED ANSARI

Law student Mahsheed was born in Afghanistan, has lived in India, and her permanent home is Australia. She is passionate about meeting, understanding, studying and working with people in order to better herself and her community.

I and all men should declare thankfully and proudly:

Sufficient for me is the One Who created me and took me out of the darkness of non-existence, bestowing on me light of being.

Likewise, sufficient for me is the One Who bestowed on me the bounty of life, which gives all things to those who possess it and stretches out its hands to all things.

Likewise, sufficient for me is the One Who made me a human being and bestowed on me the bounty of humanity, which makes man the microcosm, greater in meaning than the macrocosm.

Likewise, sufficient for me is the One Who made me a believer and bestowed on me the bounty of belief, which makes this world and the hereafter two tables laden with bounties, and offers them to the believer with the hand of belief.

Likewise, sufficient for me is the One Who made me a member of the community of His Beloved, Muhammad (Peace and blessings be upon him) and bestowed on me love of God and being loved by Him, which are found in belief and are the highest degrees of human perfection; and through this love springing from belief, expanded the extent to which believers could benefit, to the infinite contents of the spheres of contingency and necessity ...

Sufficient for me is my Sustainer; May God be exalted!

My heart's inner life is the remembrance of God;

The remembrance of Ahmad; God's blessings be upon him!

There is no god but God!

Bediuzzaman Said Nursi

Reflections

This prayer came to my aid when I was going through a troublesome time. It acts as a reminder and a revelation that truly God only is sufficient for us, and that nothing, no-one and no matter can ever fulfil and satisfy us save God alone. I often read this passage by Muslim scholar Said Nursi, who himself was suffering and lonely when he wrote it.

This prayer is especially relevant at times when we feel that no-one really understands us or appreciates us, so that we feel limited, insignificant and finite. It consoles us by reassuring us that belief in God adds value to all creation, even to our ephemeral limited self. This prayer quenches my thirst for infinity through connecting me to an eternal divine being; it eases my wounds and reminds me of the beauty and artistry in all things, even in our current state of affairs. For me the prayer has a magical effect that gives me inner self contentment.

I think all Australians can relate to the essence of this passage – that through a close connection with God or the Divine Holy One, we can attain the inner peace, confidence and motivation which are vital for the spiritual wellbeing of our country.

Passage 'Fourth Ray: Fifth Point' from 'The Rays' collection, in Bediuzzaman Said Nursi, *Risale-i Nur*, Sözler Publications, Istanbul, 2002.
Bediuzzaman Said Nursi (1876–1960), was a highly regarded scholar. *The Risale-i Nur* was a 6000-page commentary on the Qur'an.

THE MOST REVEREND DOCTOR
PHILLIP ASPINALL
ARCHBISHOP OF BRISBANE

A science graduate from the University of Tasmania, Phillip worked as a computer programmer, youth worker and Christian educator before undertaking postgraduate studies in theology and education and business administration. He was elected Archbishop of Brisbane in 2002, and in 2005, he became primate of the Anglican Church of Australia.

Love is born
With a dark and troubled face
When hope is dead
And in the most unlikely place
Love is born:
Love is always born.

Michael Leunig

God help us to live slowly:
To move simply:
To look softly:
To allow emptiness:
To let the heart create for us.

Amen.

Michael Leunig

Reflections

Michael Leunig is an insightful and spiritually awake cartoonist and theologian. His prayers and reflections are simple and moving. They open the heart and mind to God, which is the essence of spirituality.

⬤ Michael Leunig, *When I Talk to You: a cartoonist talks to God*, HarperCollins, Sydney, 2004.

ADUT DAU ATEM

A Sudanese-born migrant, Adut is studying medical science at the University of Canberra. Her role as a special youth representative for the United Nations High Commissioner for Refugees (UNHCR) enables her to let young Australians know that women and children are the real victims of war.

> Even if you are starving, you must never ever steal anyone else's food, no matter how hungry you are. If you do not have food yourself, then you are meant to be starving. Be patient, your time will come. It is never acceptable to take what isn't yours.
>
> Dau Atem Yong

Reflections

These are the words of my father. When the bombs went off in our school and I become separated from my family, he was a political prisoner. Later, when he was released from prison, he walked for two years trying to relocate his family, who were scattered all over the Sudan. I'd been at a refugee camp, on the Kenyan border, for four years when he walked into our camp. By then I was thirteen years old. I'd thought he was dead. It is hard to describe what it was like living in a crowded refugee camp with 90,000 other people. We were given one cup of maize and some oil to eat every two weeks. We had to walk a long way for water and we brought it back in big buckets. When there was no food, we called those days 'black days'. My father would sit us down on the dry dirt with the dry wind blowing in that place where there was no hope, hold us together and speak strongly to our souls, encouraging us to believe we could be anything we dreamed we could be. His words became an echo inside me, helping me to find strength when I had none. He would encourage us to go to the little school at the camp, even when we couldn't concentrate. He loved us, and we knew and felt it.

He organised a sponsorship for my siblings and me to come to Australia. Two years later they found my mother, whom we'd thought to be dead. We hadn't seen her for eleven years; he hadn't seen her for fifteen. He died two days after she arrived in Australia. His strong spirit is still with me, guiding me and encouraging me to keep going. I miss him terribly.

● Adut is also mentioned in Naomi Steer's contribution on page 171 and Sophie Weldon's contribution on pages 186–187.

THE REVEREND CANON DOCTOR
STUART BARTON BABBAGE, AM

Former dean of St Andrew's Cathedral, Sydney, and dean of St Paul's Cathedral, Melbourne, Stuart has also been the principal of theological colleges in Australia and the United States. While following his passion for social justice, he met US civil rights activist Martin Luther King Jr on several occasions.

> Lord Jesus, Master, carpenter of Nazareth, who through nails and wood wrought man's redemption on the cross, wield well thy tools in this thy workshop, that we, who come to thee rough hewn, may be fashioned into instruments for the fulfilment of thy purpose, who with the Father and the Holy Spirit liveth and reigneth one God, for ever and ever.
>
> Amen.
>
> **Anonymous**

Reflections

I like the way in which this passage uses the symbolism of the carpenter's shop imaginatively and devotionally.

OOO

MARGOT BABER

In January 2001 Margot's life was shattered when her husband was brutally murdered. Her friendships, faith and love of life have propelled the part-time midwife and antenatal educator through her journey of grief, allowing her to find peace, love and happiness through adversity.

I no longer felt its beat inside of me,
But instead there was a gaping hole in my chest.
He held part of me in the palm of his hands,
And it would be his forever; there was no way of getting it back.
From that day on I lived in darkness
With the main part of my life missing.
The clouds were always dark and grey,
And the rain fell down my cheeks.
I looked back and wished I did it differently,
I would have taken it all back.
Sorry. Sorry, I would have told you that night,
But what I said is done.
I woke this morning and looked out the window,
Tears were falling from the skies.
I walked the streets,
While people whispered
But all my senses had gone.
They talked but I could not hear,
They made gestures, but I was blind;
But no one asked me questions although I was willing.
Years went by but not much changed,
I still think of you each day.
I'm not the only one affected by this,
But without them I would be nothing ...
I woke one morning to see blue skies,

continued overleaf

The sun shone greater than ever;
The life I was living was taking yet another twist
And this time the future looked bright.
Places were changed,
Additions were made,
And compromises were in place.
We grew in number,
Yet bigger the better
And I couldn't wish to be any happier.
You'd be pleased to know
That with a new family, yes we are together.
But as life goes on we don't forget;
As memories are forever.

Bonnie Duncan

Reflections

On 24 January 2001, my beautiful husband would have gently kissed me goodbye so as not to wake me before he left for work. By lunchtime he had been brutally murdered and my world now existed without him. He never had the opportunity to say farewell to his four children, all were under eleven years old. This poem, 'Memories are Forever', was written five years after he died by my daughter, Bonnie.

● Bonnie Duncan, (1990-), *Memories are Forever.*

HIS EMINENCE ARCHBISHOP
AGHAN BALIOZIAN, OAM

Aghan Baliozian has been primate of the Diocese of the Armenian Church of Australia and New Zealand since 1981. He is also actively involved in ecumenical life through the National Council of Churches in Australia and international inter-faith dialogues.

O light, Creator of Light; Primeval Light; who dwells in inaccessible light; O Heavenly Father, blessed by the orders of the shining Angels at the dawn of this morning's light; shed forth into our souls Your Spiritual Light.

Of Light from Light: Sun of Righteousness, Son of the Father, who is the Ineffable Offspring, whose Name is hymned with the Father before the rising of the sun at dawn of this morning's light: shed forth into our souls Your Spiritual Light.

O Light proceeding from the Father: You Holy Spirit: God, Fountain of Goodness: the children of the Church together with the angels praise You at the dawn of this morning's light: shed forth into our souls Your Spiritual Light.

O Light Triune: Indivisible Holy Trinity, we sons of earth, together with the heavenly ones, ever glorify You at the dawn of the morning's light: shed forth into our souls Your Spiritual Light.

Nerses Shnorhali

Reflections

In the Armenian Apostolic Church this hymn forms part of the morning prayer service reserved for the Lenten period. It is, however, a favourite daily reflection of mine with which I start each day. It inspires me to seek and feel the presence of God from the moment I open my eyes until the end of the day. This inspiration is founded in the Light of God the Father, confirmed by the Light of his son Jesus Christ and revealed in the Light of the Holy Spirit. It reminds me of the need to depend on the Holy Trinity to guide my daily life.

● Nerses Shnorhali (1100–1173), or 'Nerses the Graceful', was Catholicos (supreme Patriarch) of Armenia from 1166–1173 and an outstanding theologian, poet, prose writer and composer of sacred music. This is one of many morning prayers he wrote.

○○○

LARISSA BEHRENDT

Born into the Eualeyai/Kamilaroi Aboriginal nations, Larissa studied law at the University of New South Wales and at Harvard Law School. She is currently professor of law and director of research at the Jumbunna Indigenous House of Learning at the University of Technology in Sydney.

> In the end, we will remember not the words of our enemies, but the silence of our friends.
>
> Martin Luther King Jr

Reflections

These words remind me that it is not good enough to stand silent when the poor, the marginalised and the disadvantaged are not able to speak out, and that we should be diligent in constantly protecting the rights of those who are less fortunate than ourselves.

● Dr Martin Luther King Jr (1929–68) was an American Baptist minister and civil rights activist.

○○○

JOHN BELL, OBE, AM

Distinguished actor, and artistic director of Bell Shakespeare, John is considered by many to be the father of Australian Shakespearean theatre. He has received many honours including an honorary doctorate of letters from the Universities of Newcastle, Sydney and New South Wales.

> **this thing of darkness I Acknowledge mine.**
>
> **William Shakespeare**

Reflections

In *The Tempest*, Prospero comes to realise that until he forgives his enemies and admits to his own frailties, he can never leave his desert island and rejoin the great stream of humanity. The play deals with letting go of rage and the desire for revenge.

❚ William Shakespeare, The Tempest, act 5, scene 1, lines 275–76.

OOO

CHARLES BIRCH

A professor of biology for twenty-five years, Charles is now emeritus professor at the University of Sydney. Through his writings, teaching and public speaking, he draws attention to the interaction of science and religion and their influence in shaping our attitudes to the world about us.

> The art of life is first to be alive, secondly to be alive in a satisfactory way and thirdly to acquire an increase in satisfaction.
>
> Alfred North Whitehead

Reflections

Alfred North Whitehead's philosophy of life has been my inspiration for many decades. This statement has a certain obviousness about it, but it has a profound meaning. The urge to live is to be alive. Lose that urge and you die. So I think it can be truly said that evolution is more than the survival of the fittest. It is the survival of those who have abundant life, with its ongoing urge to discover that from which we feel separated. The urge to live has three components: creative activity, self-fulfilment with its self-enjoyment, and aim. Every moment some new experience is achieved. That depends upon the focus provided by aim. Each moment of self-fulfilment itself extends the aim.

● Excerpt from Alfred North Whitehead, *The Function of Reason*, ©1929 Princeton University Press.
AN Whitehead (1861–1947) was a British scientist and philosopher.

○○○

VERONICA BRADY

For many years Sister Veronica has worked in the academic field, one of the first Australian nuns to do so. A member of the Institute of the Blessed Virgin Mary (the Loreto Sisters), she is deeply concerned with issues of justice and peace, particularly regarding reconciliation with Aboriginal Australians.

The Lord is my shepherd, I shall not want;
he makes me lie down in green pastures. He leads me
beside still waters;
he restores my soul. He leads me in paths of righteousness
for his name's sake.

Even though I walk through the valley of the shadow of
death, I fear no evil; for thou art with me; thy rod and thy
staff, they comfort me.

Thou preparest a table before me in the presence of my
enemies; thou anointest my head with oil, my cup
overflows.

Surely goodness and mercy shall follow me all the days
of my life; and I shall dwell in the house of the Lord
for ever.

Psalm 23 Revised Standard Version Bible

Reflections

I first read this psalm in my twenties in a Melbourne park in springtime. I was confused and wondering what to do in my life. It has always inspired me with a vision of a presence who gives life, always goes ahead of my ways and leads me along ways I can trust, however confusing or painful they may be.

OOO

AJAHN BRAHM

London-born Ajahn studied theoretical physics prior to being ordained as a Buddhist monk in Thailand. Currently he is abbot of the Bodhinyana Buddhist Monastery in Perth. His book *Opening the Door of Your Heart* has been published in ten languages.

An uneducated old man was visiting a city for the first time in his life. He had grown up in a remote mountain village, worked hard raising his children, and was now enjoying his first visit to his children's modern homes. One day, while being shown around the city, the old man heard a sound that stung his ears. He had never heard such an awful noise in his quiet mountain village and he insisted on finding its cause. Following the grating sound back to its source, he came to a room in the back of a house where a small boy was practising on a violin.

Screech! Scrape! came the discordant notes from the groaning instrument.

When he was told by his son that that was called a 'violin', he decided he never wanted to hear such a horrible thing again.

The next day, in a different part of the city, the old man heard a sound that seemed to caress his aged ears. He had never heard such an enchanting melody in his mountainous valley, so he demanded to find its cause. Following the delightful sound back to its source, he came to a room in the front of a house where an old lady, a maestro, was performing a sonata on a violin.

At once, the old man realised his mistake. The terrible sound that he had heard the previous day was not the fault of the violin, nor even of the boy. It was just that the young man had yet to learn his instrument well.

The old man thought it was the same with religion. When we come across a religious enthusiast causing such strife with his beliefs, it is incorrect to blame the religion. It is just that the novice has yet to learn his religion well. When we come across a saint, a maestro of her religion, it is such a sweet encounter that it inspires us for many years, whatever their beliefs.

... but that was not the end of the story of the old man and the violin. The third day, in a different part of the city, the old man heard another sound that surpassed in its beauty and purity even that of the maestro on her violin. What do you think that sound was?

It was a sound more beautiful than the cascade of the mountain stream in spring, than the autumn wind through forest groves, or than the mountain birds singing after a heavy rain. It was even more beautiful than the silence in the mountain hollows on a still winter's night. What was that sound that moved the old man's heart more powerfully than anything before?

It was a large orchestra playing a symphony.

The reason it was the most beautiful sound in the world was, firstly, that every member of that orchestra was a maestro of their own instrument; and secondly, that they had further learned how to play together in harmony.

'May it be the same with religion,' the old man thought. 'Let each one of us learn through the lessons of life the soft heart of our beliefs. Let us each be a maestro of the love within our religion. Then, having learned our religion well, let us go further and learn how to play, like members of an orchestra, with other religions in harmony together!' That would be the most beautiful sound.

Ajahn Brahm

Reflections

There is no greater evil, I think, than the violence between peoples, and much of this stems from religion. The story of 'the most beautiful sound' shows a model whereby we can each maintain our own faith, yet still work together for something even higher. It is a simple story of hope in a time of fear.

Excerpt from Ajahn Brahm, *Opening the Door of Your Heart*, Hachette Livre Australia, Sydney, 2004. Reprinted with permission.

PROFESSOR
JENNIE BRAND-MILLER

Jennie is an internationally renowned scientist. She is especially recognised for her groundbreaking work on the glycaemic index, a method of measuring the body's absorption of carbohydrates. In 2003, Jennie won the Clunies Ross Medal for contributions to science and technology in Australia. Jennie overcame deafness in her younger days and has two bionic ear implants.

Michael Leunig

Reflections

This Leunig cartoon representing life's ups and downs rings very true for me. I recognised this cyclical nature of life's events as a teenager. No matter how bad things seem, we can rely on the knowledge that the feelings are temporary and that good will always follow bad. I show this cartoon to my students and colleagues when they need cheering up. Look closely – I'm in awe of how Leunig has been able to infuse his little people with so much emotion, both happy and sad. The power of a cartoon! I often think of it.

○○○

FATHER
FRANK BRENNAN, sj, ao

A Jesuit priest, lawyer and author, Frank is a professor of law, human rights and social justice at two Catholic universities in Australia. His views are informed by his experience with Aboriginal people, refugees and those whose call for justice is judged by the powerful to be inopportune or inconvenient.

> Here is my servant whom I uphold, my chosen one in whom my soul delights. I have endowed him with my spirit that he may bring true justice to the nations.
>
> He does not cry out or shout aloud, or make his voice heard in the streets. He does not break the crushed reed, nor quench the wavering flame.
>
> Faithfully he brings true justice; he will neither waver, nor be crushed until true justice is established on earth, for the islands are awaiting his law.
>
> Isaiah, 42:1–4 Jerusalem Bible

Reflections

I joined the Jesuit Order in 1975 when there was a strong emphasis in the Order on the relationship between faith and justice. I had just completed my university studies in law and politics. I then had two years' novitiate, developing my prayer life and reflecting on what God asked of me. My superiors asked me to consider the plight of Aboriginal Australians. I experienced a strong call to go deeper into myself, and to reach out more in the world; to practise law and politics while being attentive to and respecting the voice, experience and wisdom of the voiceless and powerless.

This prayer of the suffering servant has always held in creative and hopeful tension for me the two worlds and the two times in which Christians are called to live, work and pray – the already, but not yet; the achievable, but impossible; the ideal and the real; working, relating and enacting the coming of the kingdom here on earth, while praying and hoping for the kingdom to come in which freedom, justice and love might survive even suffering and death, forever.

OOO

TRISHA BROADBRIDGE

Trisha lost her husband, Troy, when the 2004 tsunami struck. The couple had been in Thailand on their honeymoon. In honour of Troy, Trisha set up the Reach Broadbridge Fund, which works to make significant and positive differences in the lives of young people in both Australia and Thailand. Trisha was Young Australian of the Year in 2006.

If I have learned one thing this past year it is that nothing in life is certain and no one has the right to judge how a person should, or shouldn't, react to tragedy. In my heart I know there is nothing extraordinary about me or anyone else who endures tragedy. In fact it is the ordinariness of all of us that should be the focus. Society's way of moving forward is to make people 'extraordinary', so that they do not have to cope with the reality of knowing that in the darkest moments, when the pain is at its most intense, sometimes all that is left is a person who feels there is no reason to stay alive. There is no flash of light or sudden realisation that life is great and you can cope. There is just a day-to-day struggle, the slow rebuilding process, the love of your friends and the indefinable human quality which enables you to take the next step.

Trisha Broadbridge and Jon Carnegie

Reflections
This is a personal reflection on my journey.

● Excerpt from Trisha Broadbridge and Jon Carnegie, *Beyond the Wave: a tsunami survivor's story*, Allen & Unwin, Sydney, 2005.

LUCINDA BRYANT, OAM

Lucinda is artistic director of Merry Makers Australia, a voluntary charitable organisation which assists people with intellectual and physical disabilities. In their performances, the sixty-five Merry Makers express themselves through music and dance, touching people's hearts and breaking down boundaries.

> We end our alienation when we discover that we are all part of the same story. Find harmony with nature and we find ourselves, and then our hearts are full. Listen to the wind and the rain. Feel the land beneath your feet. Stand naked in the rays of our sun. We are all stardust.
>
> Jeff McMullen

Reflections

I admire Jeff McMullen (see his entry on page 118) and aspire to be like him. I find that particular quotation truly inspirational. It has a beautiful link to nature, which I am passionate about. It also reinforces that we are all part of one great world, which we need to share and respect.

Jeff wrote a personal note for me in the front of the book: 'Every breath can make a difference, as you have already found. If you keep believing that we can move the world, we will.' His words remind me of our potential and inspire me to be a better person.

● Excerpt from Jeff McMullen, *A Life of Extremes: journeys and encounters*, HarperCollins, Sydney, 2001.

ANDREW BUCHANAN

A prominent communications and media consultant, Andrew has had a long career in broadcasting. While general manager of the ABC's international development area, he led training consultancies in Vietnam, Laos, Cambodia and South Africa. Shortly after he was born, Andrew contracted polio which left him paralysed on his right side.

> This book went to press at the start of a war that will have global reverberations for years to come. These are times when we will need all our resilience: at home with those we love, in communities which may be divided, abroad in a world made fearful, in our relationships with nations that may not share our views.
>
> Resilience is about facing adversity with hope. We inhabit one world in which we are all deeply connected. I hope for the wisdom and justice which will bring us peace.
>
> Anne Deveson

Reflections

To inspire is a rare gift and I have always admired those who have that ability to make us think and achieve through their influence. Interestingly, the Oxford Dictionary defines 'inspire' as to breathe in air, or infuse thought or feeling into a person.

Apart from my family, two individuals who have inspired me during my career in broadcasting and communication – and in more recent years, in the challenging field of the disability sector – are Australian journalist, broadcaster and film-maker Anne Deveson, and Nelson Mandela.

On several occasions in the mid-1960s, Anne interviewed me regarding my attitude to growing up with a disability in both a small country school and at a Sydney boarding school. Anne's films have won UN Media Peace awards and her moving book, *Tell Me I'm Here*, outlined her son's challenges with schizophrenia. I have a family member with this form of mental illness and, as with all aspects of disability, one needs oodles of resilience, and a sense of humour never goes astray!

In her book, *Resilience*, Anne asks the question, how is it that some people can be resilient in adversity while others become overwhelmed? To say the least, Anne Deveson exemplifies resilience.

Working with the ABC in Cambodia in 1997, I was enthralled to read the autobiography of Nelson Mandela, who I believe is a true leader with outstanding moral and political skills. I found interesting parallels between Mandela's struggle and the struggle of Cambodians during the Pol Pot regime.

My daughters advise me that many of us possess natural physical ability, but it is the power of the mind and the imagination that ultimately determines success. Our heart, mind, body and soul are four essentials of human endeavour, but it is the attention that we give to developing each that determines priorities in our lives.

Excerpt from Anne Deveson, *Resilience*, Allen & Unwin, Sydney, 2003.

LINDA BURNEY

Linda is a member of the Wiradjuri nation. In 2003, she became the first Indigenous woman to be elected into the New South Wales Parliament. She has a high profile at state and national levels in education and training as well as in Aboriginal affairs. In 2007 Linda was appointed Minister for Youth, Volunteering and Fair Trade.

If I speak in the tongues of mortals and of angels, but do not have love, I am a noisy gong or a clanging cymbal.

And if I have prophetic powers, and understand all mysteries and all knowledge, and if I have all faith, so as to remove mountains, but do not have love, I am nothing.

If I give away all my possessions, and if I hand over my body so that I may boast, but do not have love, I gain nothing.

continued overleaf

Love is patient; love is kind; love is not envious or boastful or arrogant or rude. It does not insist on its own way; it is not irritable or resentful; it does not rejoice in wrongdoing, but rejoices in the truth.

It bears all things, believes all things, hopes all things, endures all things.

Love never ends. But as for prophecies, they will come to an end; as for tongues, they will cease; as for knowledge, it will come to an end.

For we know only in part, and we prophesy only in part; but when the complete comes, the partial will come to an end.

When I was a child, I spoke like a child, I thought like a child, I reasoned like a child; when I became an adult, I put an end to childish ways.

For now we see in a mirror, dimly, but then we will see face to face. Now I know only in part; then I will know fully, even as I have been fully known.

And now faith, hope, and love abide, these three; and the greatest of these is love.

I Corinthians 13, New Revised Standard Version Bible

Reflections

This verse was read out at the funeral of a relative. The words touched me deeply as my husband, Rick, lay desperately ill in hospital – he has since passed on as well. This verse talks about deep love, the kind that Rick and I had shared.

JULIAN BURNSIDE, QC

Author and human rights advocate, Julian Burnside is known for his opposition to the mandatory detention of asylum seekers, and has appeared as counsel in various prominent cases. Julian declares that he is a barrister, a sceptic and optimist despite everything.

> **All men should strive to learn before they die what they are running from, and to, and why.**
>
> James Thurber

Reflections

Thurber wrote a series called *Fables for Our Time*. He was writing during the time of Joe McCarthy's anti-communist witch-hunts, and cloaked his message in the friendly, familiar form of *Aesop's Fables*. He used the benign innocence of furry animals as a vehicle for criticism of tyranny and stupidity, just as Aesop had done. The last of his fables concerns lemmings, and the helpless despair of a philosopher-lemming who watches, in perplexity, as his fellow lemmings throw themselves over the cliff ('some crying "we are lost", some crying "we are saved" …'). The quotation I've chosen is the moral to the story. It is profoundly true.

● Excerpt from James Thurber, The Shore and the Sea in *Further Fables for our Time*, Simon & Schuster, New York, 1956. James Thurber (1894–1961) was a US cartoonist and humourist.

HELEN CALDICOTT

Nobel Peace Prize nominee Helen Caldicott is a paediatrician, author and teacher. In 2006, the Peace Organisation of Australia presented Helen with the inaugural Australian Peace Prize for her 'longstanding commitment to raising awareness about the medical and environmental hazards of the nuclear age'.

My connection with the beyond comes from nature. I am a pantheist, and nature for me is holy and sacred. My most important insights and inspirations come when I am alone and quiet in the garden with the pelicans circling high overhead.

Helen Caldicott

Reflections

In a world obsessed with anthropogenic religion, it is important to keep observations simple. That's why nature teaches us all the lessons that we need to know – birth, beauty, diversity, reproduction and death.

PETER CARROLL

An actor of many years standing, and winner of numerous awards, Peter was educated by the Marist Brothers, the Universities of Sydney and New South Wales, and at the Central School of Speech and Drama in London.

Put on the garments that suit God's chosen people, His own, His beloved and those garments are compassion, kindness, humility, gentleness, patience. Be forbearing with one another and forgiving. Where any of you has cause for complaint you must forgive as the Lord forgave you and to crown all there must be love. To bind all together and to complete the whole, let Christ's peace be arbiter in your hearts. For to this peace you were all called as members of a single body.

Colossians 3:12–15

Reflections

Acting is prayer. Text, voice, movement and costume are all part of liturgy. Forgiveness is possibly the most important idea for me.

● Excerpt from *Silence and Stillness in Every Season: daily readings with John Main*, ed. Paul Harris, Dartman Longman & Todd, London, 1997. Reprinted by permission of The Continuum International Publishing Group.

John Main (1926–82) was a Benedictine monk and founder of the World Community for Christian Meditation.

○○○

TAMSIN CARROLL

Tamsin has worked in the entertainment industry for over two decades, performing as a singer and actor in a variety of genres. She won a Helpmann Award in 2006 for best female actor in the highly successful musical *Dusty*.

What a piece of work is man
How noble in reason
How infinite in faculties
In form and moving
How express and admirable
In action how like an angel
In apprehension how like a god
The beauty of the world
The paragon of animals

I have of late
But wherefore I know not
Lost all my mirth
This goodly frame
The earth
Seems to me a sterile promontory
This most excellent canopy
The air – look you!
This brave o'erhanging firmament
This majestical roof
Fretted with golden fire
Why it appears no other thing to me
Than a foul and pestilent congregation
Of vapors

What a piece of work is man
How noble in reason

How dare they try to end this beauty?
How dare they try to end this beauty?

Walking in space
We find the purpose of peace
The beauty of life
You can no longer hide

Our eyes are open
Our eyes are open
Our eyes are open
Our eyes are open
Wide wide wide!

James Rado and Gerome Ragni

Reflections

This was always a show-stopper for me. A moment to really reflect on the equality of man even with all the beautiful differences that accompany us! Shakespeare always puts it best! A time to question why on earth we fight our diversity, when it is exactly what we should celebrate.

From the musical *Hair*, 'What a Piece of Work is Man', lyrics by James Rado and Gerome Ragni, music by Galt Macdermot © EMU Catalog Inc. Reproduced by permission of Alfred Publishing (Australia) Pty Ltd.
The lyrics of 'What a Piece of Work is Man' were inspired by lives from William Shakesphere's tragedy, *Hamlet* (2:2:115–17).

IDRIS EDWARD CASSIDY

Cardinal Cassidy's appointments have included Vatican Diplomatic Corps, president of the Pontifical Council for Promoting Christian Unity, under secretary of state in the Roman Curia, cardinal deacon of Santa Maria in Via Lata, and General Secretariat's Council for the Special Assembly of the Bishops' Synod for Lebanon.

Out of the depths I cry to you, O Lord
Lord, hear my voice!
O let your ears be attentive
To the voice of my pleading.

If you, O Lord, should mark our guilt,
Lord, who would survive?
But with you is found forgiveness:
For this we revere you.

My soul is waiting for the Lord
I count on his word.
My soul is longing for the Lord
More than watchman for daybreak.
Let the watchman count on daybreak
And Israel on the Lord.

Because with the Lord there is mercy
And fullness of redemption,
Israel indeed will he redeem
From all its iniquity.

Psalm 130

Reflections

There are so many prayers a priest offers each day that it is hard to select one which means the most to me. One psalm I always return to with a deep feeling of joy and comfort is the *De Profundis* Psalm 130.

Another short prayer I say frequently that keeps me in touch with the Lord as I go daily about other things in his service is, 'Lord Jesus Christ, son of the living God, have mercy on me, I put my trust in you!'

Finally, there is a motto I chose when I became a bishop that has strengthened me ever since: *Deus, fortitudo mea* – The Lord is my strength.

● Psalm 130, from *The Grail*, Collins, London, 1963. Reprinted by permission of HarperCollins Publishers Ltd ©1963.

○○○

FULYA CELIK

Sydney-born Fulya combines journalism, religious studies and educational projects in her work towards inter-faith relations. She was recently involved in the Building Bridges Project, which brought together Muslim and Jewish families, and she is a passionate volunteer with the Australian Intercultural Society.

O One All-Knowing of the Unseen;
O One Ever-Forgiving of sins;
O Veiler of faults;
O Dispeller of grief;
O Overturner of hearts;
O Adorner of hearts;
O Illuminator of hearts;
O Physician of hearts;
O Beloved of hearts;
O Intimate of hearts –

Glory be unto Thee, Thou art without
Partner or fault! There is no god but Thee!
Mercy, mercy, deliver us from Hell-fire!

Al-Jawshan al-Kabir

Reflections

'Al-Jawshan al-Kabir' is a prayer most frequently recited by Muslims. It is a long prayer consisting of one hundred chapters, and nearly all chapters, with a few exceptions, consist of ten of God's names and attributes.

The twelfth chapter describes God Almighty as the sole source of sanctuary – One in whom all beings seek refuge – the Owner of Hearts. This section echoes the sorrow of a burning heart and serves as its panacea. These lines also illustrate the innate purpose of the human heart to act as a mirror reflecting the Beautiful Names of God Almighty.

The secrets contained within the heart are unlocked by Divine Love. This chapter reveals that it is through the heart that one can form an intimate connection with God.

Hidden within the words of this supplication is the lamenting of a heart which, in turn, mirrors the sorrow of my own heart. It is through a spiritual knowledge of God that the heart can find solace. As such, the meaning in 'dispeller of grief' becomes manifest.

This chapter, for me, symbolises the yearning felt by the heart in its search of its beloved and represents the sorrow felt because of its separation. It too offers a refuge from loneliness and despair. Fethullah Gulen, a contemporary Islamic scholar from Turkey, who places importance on reciting verses from 'Al-Jawshan al-Kabir', states: 'The Almighty considers hearts, not outward appearances or forms. Among hearts, He considers the sad and broken ones and honors their owners with His presence.' (M. Fethullah Gulen, *Key Concepts in the Practice of Sufism*, The Light Publishing, 2006, vol. 1, p. 30.)

● Excerpt from the twelfth chapter of 'Al-Jawshan al-Kabir', in *A Prayer for All: supplication of Prophet Muhammad*, Sözler Publications, Istanbul, 2003.
  'Al-Jawshan al-Kabir' is derived from the Qur'an and is one of the many prayers of supplication from the Prophet Muhammad.

○○○

LINDY CHAMBERLAIN-CREIGHTON

Lindy Chamberlain will always be associated with the 1980 death of her nine-and-a-half-week old baby, Azaria. Lindy, author of her own biography, is now a public speaker on the law, media; prison life; grief, loss and forgiveness; family life and personal responsibility. Her wrongful conviction for murder was quashed in 1988.

> Nothing before, nothing behind;
> the steps of Faith
> Fall on the seeming void, and find
> the rock beneath.
>
> John Greenleaf Whittier

Reflections

God is my rock, he will never let me down. Even if he says no, or wait a while, I know he has something better in mind if I will wait patiently.

Sometimes we have a tendency to blame God, when in fact God is the only one we can rely on to see us through. God is not the cause of pain, grief or loss. He gave his life just so that there was a future for us without suffering. Knowing God loved us that much, why do we blame him and not trust him with all our heart and life?

No matter what happens to us we can handle it with God by our side, and even if we would not choose that way to learn, trouble can teach us some of the best lessons of our lives that we would refuse to learn otherwise. With trust and faith in God we can do anything.

● Excerpt from John Greenleaf Whittier, *My Soul and I*.
John Greenleaf Whittier (1807–92) was a Quaker poet and journalist and a leading opponent of slavery.

◯◯◯

TAGHRED CHANDAB

A journalist for the *Sun-Herald,* Taghred is the award-winning co-author of *The Glory Garage: growing up Lebanese Muslim in Australia.* Through her writing, Taghred hopes to continue to educate the wider community about Islam. She lives with her family in Sydney.

> A woman as a mother commands great respect in Islam.
> A man once asked the Prophet Muhammad (peace be upon him): 'O Messenger of Allah, who is the person who has the greatest right on me with regards to kindness and attention?'
> He replied, 'Your mother.'
> 'Then who?'
> He replied, 'Your mother.'
> 'Then who?'
> He replied, 'Your mother.'
> 'Then who?'
> He replied, 'Your mother.'
> The Prophet states emphatically that the rights of a mother are paramount.
>
> **Prophet Muhammad**

Reflections

I chose this passage because for me it is a daily reminder of the kindness and love we must all show our mothers. So often mothers are taken for granted and it is not until we are going through personal struggles or suffering from an illness that we realise how comforting it is when we are with them. Mothers sacrifice so much for their children, and as adults we must make sacrifices to make sure our mother is protected and loved unconditionally.

The Prophet Muhammad advised one of his believers not to join the war against the Quraish (non-believers) in defence of Islam, but to look after his mother, saying that his service to his mother would be a cause of his salvation. He said: 'Remain in your mother's service because Paradise is under her feet.'

● Excerpt from Abdul Rahman I Doi, *Women in the Qur'an and the Sunnah*, Taha Publishers Ltd, London, 1993.
Dr Abdul Rahman I Doi (1933–99) was an expert on Islamic education and Islam in Africa.

GRAEME CLARK, AC

Motivated by his father's deafness, Graeme developed the cochlear implant (bionic ear), an electronic device that restores partial hearing to the deaf. Over the last thirty years, more than 80,000 people around the world have been fitted with the bionic ear. Graeme was Senior Australian of the Year in 2001.

> For who makes you different from anyone else? What do you have that you did not receive? And if you did receive it, why do you boast as though you did not?
>
> I Corinthians 4:7 New International Version Bible

Reflections

This was a favourite quote of Denis Burkitt, the pioneer and medical missionary who discovered Burkitt's lymphoma.

This passage reflects the fact that we depend on others for achievements, not just our innate abilities. It also reminds me that all our gifts do not belong to us and should be used to glorify God.

OOO

KAREENA CLIFFORD

Born in Guyana, South America, Kareena is now a Queenslander. For over a decade she has been working with new and emerging communities in the area of social justice. Kareena has received numerous awards for her support and advancement of multiculturalism and harmony within the community.

It doesn't take much
to hold the tiny weight
of a song sparrow,
any little twig will do,
or a sturdy weed in a field.

Why do I think my fledging ideas
have to wait for a thick branch
or a secure landing place
before I set them down?

The wisp of a fleeting dream
can rest for a while
on a small extension in my soul.

If I never let these dreams land,
they will not gain strength
for the long flight into fullness.

All it takes is a little twig
to rest a great dream on.

Joyce Rupp

Reflections

Working in an environment where the needs of the people we work with are great and resources are extremely limited, this poem reminds me of the importance of giving wings to dreams and having the courage to step out in faith.

● Excerpt from Joyce Rupp and Barbara Lewis, *Rest Your Dreams on a Little Twig*, used with permission of Sorin Books. Text ©2003 Joyce Rupp, art ©2003 Barbara Lewis. Sorin Books is an imprint of Ave Maria Press.
   Joyce Rupp (1943–) is a Servite sister and describes herself as a spiritual midwife.

PAUL COLEMAN SJ

For more than forty years Father Paul has been working in parishes, including nine years as chaplain at Mary MacKillop Place in North Sydney. There he encountered a great variety of people seeking the intercessory assistance of Mary MacKillop.

He sustained him in a desert land,
in a howling wilderness waste;
he shielded him, cared for him,
guarded him as the apple of his eye.

As an eagle stirs up its nest,
and hovers over its young;
as it spreads its wings, takes them up,
and bears them aloft on its pinions.

The Lord alone guided him;
no foreign god was with him.

Deuteronomy 32:10–12 New Revised Standard Version Bible

Reflections

I find this passage very reassuring and comforting.

ROGER CORBETT, AM

Roger has had a distinguished career in retailing, from working on the dock of Grace Bros in Sydney to serving as chief executive officer of Woolworths Ltd. His many awards include the B'nai B'rith (Australia–New Zealand) Gold Medal in 2006. Roger is on the board of directors of the Reserve Bank of Australia and of Fairfax Holdings Ltd.

> **For God so loved the world that he gave his only Son, that whoever believes in him should not perish but have eternal life.**
>
> **John 3:16 New Revised Standard Version Bible**

Reflections

To me the proposition that there is no God, and that the human and animal species that live on earth just happened, is beyond belief. The beauty and balance of creation can only be explained, in my view, by the existence of a creator, and therefore a God.

Given this proposition, we see the world expressing its need to worship in many ways. Under the aegis of history, this invaluable need of humankind has endured.

Where does one meet this God? For me this is best described in this passage from St John's gospel. That is the place where I met my God, and from that place my relationship with him has grown, acknowledging this 'omnipresence' and his great love for his creation, of which I am part.

○○○

TIM COSTELLO, AO

National president of the Baptist Union of Australia from 1999 to 2002, Tim has long been a voice of social conscience on issues such as global poverty, gambling, homelessness, reconciliation and substance abuse. He is currently the chief executive of World Vision Australia.

O Lord, make me an instrument of thy peace!
Where there is hatred, let me sow love.
Where there is injury, pardon.
Where there is discord, harmony.
Where there is doubt, faith.
Where there is despair, hope.
Where there is darkness, light.
Where there is sorrow, joy.

Oh Divine Master, grant that I may not
so much seek to be consoled as to console;
to be understood as to understand;
to be loved as to love;
for it is in giving that we receive;
it is in pardoning that we are pardoned;
and it is in dying that we are born to eternal life.

Attributed to St Francis of Assisi

Reflections

I use this prayer frequently, both personally and in leading church services. It is associated with St Francis because it was published on a card with his portrait. But apparently it was written in 1912 in France by a priest. It was widely circulated during the First World War. It is this historic context – 'the war to end all wars' which makes its words most meaningful as a plea for courage, hope and love in the most difficult of human situations. The emphasis on seeking the welfare of others instead of pure self-interest also stands in stark contrast to the mood of modern times.

This passage, often known as the 'Prayer of St Francis' or 'Prayer for Peace', was also chosen by other contributors, including Father Chris Riley (see his entry on page 162) and The Right Reverend Keith Slater (see his entry page 176), both of whom have made the following observations:

FATHER CHRIS RILEY, SDB

This prayer is very powerful as everything in it rings true. It is recited by Buddhist children in Japan, Tibetan monks in India, Muslims in Cairo, Christian popes in Rome and base communities in Latin America. It has been used by workers during demonstrations and strikes. It articulates our greatest need and communicates from the heart.

In most religions, 'Lord' is the most common name to express reverence for the originating fount of all being, God. My work overseas, particularly with the Muslim community, has opened up a whole new understanding of faith and religion. For world peace, we need to put aside our differences and embrace our common humanity.

THE RIGHT REVEREND KEITH SLATER

This prayer is often known as the 'Prayer of St Francis', but does not appear in the corpus of what is recorded as Francis' writings. Even so, it is in the vein of his living out the gospel and was probably written by someone inspired by Francis' spirituality.

It expresses for me something of the 'life in Christ' to which I am called to live, inspired by the example of St Francis. Through Francis I am able to see Jesus more clearly and am drawn into the heart of Jesus.

The prayer, as it is headed above, 'Prayer for Peace,' speaks to me about 'how' we live out peace in a fragmented world. It speaks to me about the expression of God's love.

St Francis, 'Prayer of St Francis'.
St Francis (1181–1226) is one of the most celebrated and best-loved saints, remembered for his gentleness and his willingness to see God's presence in all aspects of nature. He is patron saint of ecologists, animals, Assisi and Italy.

CAMILLA COWLEY

When her family's long-held Queensland sheep and cattle property came under a native title claim in 1996, Camilla helped register a co-existence agreement on the title. This enshrines the right of the elders of the Gunggari People to determine access for traditional purposes and to name the area.

> Is not this the sort of fast that pleases me
> – it is the Lord Yahweh who speaks –
> to break unjust fetters
> and undo the thongs of the yoke,
> to let the oppressed go free,
> and break every yoke,
> to share the bread with the hungry,
> and shelter the homeless poor ...
>
> Isaiah 58:6–7 Jerusalem Bible

Reflections

Isaiah offers much inspiration for a life journey underpinned by the Christian call for social justice. Verses like Isaiah 56, 'Maintain justice and do what is right', and Isaiah 58:6, have been for me a road map for living. Isaiah helps me reflect on those who are oppressed or hunger for justice in Australia, such as the first Australians, whose life choices and outcomes are limited, and those in mandatory detention seeking asylum.

OOO

THE REVEREND
BILL CREWS, AM

In 1969 a visit to the Wayside Chapel in Kings Cross changed Bill's life. Now a minister of the Ashfield Uniting Church, the former microelectronic researcher works tirelessly to assist the homeless, abandoned youth and other people in need. The Exodus Foundation, which he founded, serves over 300 meals a day to the hungry.

> Our Father who art in heaven,
> hallowed be thy name.
> Thy kingdom come,
> thy will be done,
> on earth, as it is in heaven.
> Give us this day our daily bread.
> And forgive us our trespasses,
> as we forgive those who trespass against us.
> And lead us not into temptation,
> but deliver us from evil.
> For thine is the kingdom,
> the power and the glory,
> for ever and ever.
> Amen.
>
> Lord's Prayer, traditional version

Reflections

People often ask me to pray for them and I usually respond, 'Let's say the Lord's Prayer together.' I find this prayer has an enormous calming influence and, in many ways, says it all. I often don't need to add anything else. When I am having a bad time I often just say this prayer like a mantra. I encourage other people to do the same and they often tell me how it helps.

In all I have ever said and done, the Lord's Prayer is the one that I find helps the most.

Both Matthew 6:9–13 and Luke 11:2–4 have versions of the Lord's Prayer – so-called because Jesus taught it to his apostles. It is also referred to as the 'Our Father' or the 'Paternoster'. The version in Matthew is much more widely said.

Interestingly, the sentence that concludes the Protestant version, ('For thine is the kingdom …') was a common doxology (Christian hymn of praise to God) or conclusion that was added sometime after the earliest known versions of the gospels of Luke and Matthew appeared.

> ● The Lord's Prayer was also chosen by Professor Gerald O'Collins (see his entry on page 136) and Frances Seen (see her entry on page 160), both of whom have made the following observations:

PROFESSOR GERALD O'COLLINS

This is the wonderful prayer that Jesus left for his followers. It is also a prayer that evokes his Jewish origins and echoes the Hebrew scriptures.

FRANCES SEEN

I love the plural yet personal influence of the Lord's Prayer. In praying 'Our Father', I am assured that his love is far-reaching, more than we can ever imagine. It is an opportunity for us all to draw near to the throne of grace. It is a prayer anyone can turn to in any situation, and can be used not only by the church but in community gatherings.

◯◯◯

MARY CROCK

A professor in the Faculty of Law at the University of Sydney, Mary's special interests are human rights, immigration and refugees. Mary helped to establish and run the Victorian Immigration Advice and Rights Centre Inc (now the Refugee and Immigration Law Centre) in Melbourne.

May the Lord show his mercy upon you;
May the light of his presence be your guide:
May he guard you and uphold you;
May his spirit be ever by your side.
When you sleep, may his angels watch over you;
When you wake, may he fill you with his grace:
May you love him and serve him all your days,
Then in heaven may you see his face.

John Rutter

Reflections

We all need a guardian angel. I find this blessing/prayer comforting when I am feeling particularly overwhelmed by life's stresses. It is also a protective and strengthening invocation for my children and the many other special people in my life.

● Excerpt from John Rutter, 'A Clare Benediction', ©1998 Oxford University Press, London. Reproduced by permission.

John Rutter (1945–) is an English composer who studied and worked at Clare College, Cambridge. There he wrote his first published compositions and conducted his first recording while still an undergraduate. He was later appointed director of music at the college. 'A Clare Benediction' is a choral work dedicated to Clare College.

OOO

BETTY CUTHBERT, MBE, AM

After winning an extraordinary four Olympic gold medals in track and field, Betty was dubbed 'The Golden Girl'. She has since faced tough challenges in her private life, including a diagnosis of multiple sclerosis and subsequent near financial ruin. The former sprinter has also survived a brain haemorrhage.

> But they that wait upon the Lord
> shall renew their strength;
> they shall mount up with wings as eagles;
> they shall run, and not be weary;
> and they shall walk, and not faint.
>
> Isaiah 40:31 King James Bible

Reflections

My grandmother told me of this verse, which came to her during the Olympic Games in 1956 when she was feeling too nervous to listen to my race. Imprinting those words on her mind gave her total peace and enabled her to enjoy listening to my race. I stand by the verse as God has always been my strength. Even though I only have the use of my left hand, I do not feel resentful.

OOO

DOCTOR
PAUL DARVENIZA

Paul was a player in the Australian rugby contingent that toured South Africa in 1969. In 1971, when the all-white Springbok team arrived in Australia, Paul and six fellow Wallabies sparked controversy by boycotting the tour. Eventually the Federal Government adopted an anti-apartheid policy.

> No man is an island, entire of itself; every man is a piece of the continent, a part of the main. If a clod be washed away by the sea, Europe is the less, as well as if a promontory were, as well as if a manor of thy friend's or of thine own were; Any man's death diminishes me, because I am involved in mankind; And therefore never send to know for whom the bells tolls; it tolls for thee.
>
> John Donne

Reflections

This poem (sermon) had a great impact on me when I read it as a young man, and for me it still holds true. We are all in the same boat.

🔴 Excerpt from John Donne, 'Meditation 17', *Devotions upon Emergent Occasions*, 1624. John Donne (1572–1631) was chief among the English metaphysical poets and a churchman famous for his spellbinding sermons.

OOO

BRUCE DAWE, AO

One of Australia's most acclaimed poets, Bruce writes extraordinary poems about ordinary subjects. In 1984 his collected edition *Sometimes Gladness* was named by the National Book Council as one of the ten best books published in Australia in the previous ten years. It is still in print.

Came in the morning early
with the usual sweet spices
the holy women hoping
somehow the heavy stone
might from their grieving hearts
be rolled away
– there in the sepulchre finding
angelic messengers telling
them that their Lord was risen,
they took up the folded linen
and began with wonder walking
into the light unfolding
of the ever-living day.

Many thousand mornings later,
and many saints the wiser,
may we from tombs of selfhood
by similar witnesses' goodness
move into the future
enlivened by its promise,
to praise and work and pray ...

Bruce Dawe

Reflections

I chose this poem because it reflects both the Jewish and Christian experience.

⬤ Bruce Dawe, 'The Morning', in *Madonna Magazine,* Jesuit Communications Australia, Victoria, June 2006.

WILLIAM DEANE, AC, KBE

From 1982 to 1995, William Deane was a justice of the High Court of Australia. From 1996 until 2001, he was Australia's twenty-second Governor-General. He is currently doing what he likes, including serving as president of Scouts Australia, patron of Youth off the Streets and Reconciliation Australia.

For I was hungry and you gave me food; I was thirsty and you gave me drink; I was a stranger and you made me welcome; naked and you clothed me, sick and you visited me, in prison and you came to see me.

Then the virtuous will say to him in reply, 'Lord, when did we see you hungry and feed you; or thirsty and give you drink?

When did we see you a stranger and make you welcome; naked and clothe you; sick or in prison and go to see you?'

And the King will answer, 'I tell you solemnly, in so far as you did this to one of the least of these brothers of mine, you did it to me'.

Matthew 25:35–40, Jerusalem Bible

Reflections

The passage says it all.

OOO

ANDREW DENTON

Andrew is one of Australia's most successful radio and television presenters. His courage, wit and compassion as an interviewer in programs such as *Enough Rope* on ABC Television, and in the Teen Cancer series, delight audiences. About himself, Andrew writes, 'I ask lots of questions and have very few answers.'

Watch your feelings; they become your thoughts.
Watch your thoughts; they become your words.
Watch your words; they become your actions.
Watch your actions; they become your habits.
Watch your habits; they become your character.
Watch your character; it becomes your destiny.

Author unknown

Reflections

I think these words are true.

OOO

CATHERINE DEVRYE

Author and speaker Catherine DeVrye is a former IBM executive and past winner of the Australian Executive Woman of the Year Award. She regularly speaks to leading organisations around the world on managing change, customer service and turning obstacles into opportunities.

Hope is what happens when you first see a light
Just a distant, small star in the darkest of night.

Hope is what happens with the first buds of spring
When dawn touches the sky or a bird spreads its wing.

Hope is what happens when a wound starts to heal
Whether skin deep or soul deep, you begin to feel real.

Hope is what happens when you're poor but not broken
There's a goldmine of dreams – just not yet awoken

Hope is what happens when someone is kind
A feeling not lost – just misplaced in your mind

Hope is what happens when war turns to peace
After everyone prayed that the fighting would cease

Hope is what happens with the smell of fresh rain
When your long drought of dreams is renewed yet again

Hope is what happens when clouds finally clear
Troubled thunder falls silent – courageous whispers you hear.

Hope is what happens when your heart skips a beat
When so least expected – a soul mate you meet

Hope is what happens when kindling ignites
You rediscover your passion that burns day and night

Hope is what happens when the pain eases a bit
And deep down inside, you find your true grit

Hope is what happens as long as we breathe
For although it takes time, the sorrow will leave

Hope is what happens long after the pain
Hope is what happens – again and again.

Yes, hope happens!

Catherine DeVrye

Reflections

On September 11, 2001, a friend phoned to say that her mother had died of cancer. Certainly, she shared compassion with thousands of people on the other side of the globe, but the loss of one life weighed far heavier on her mind. To her, talk of 'the world changing' was more than a media cliché – the world always changes – but her own life had tumbled and changed irrevocably with the death of the one person who had always been central to her life.

Have you ever lost hope? Was it the loss of a loved one? Are you worried by lost health or wealth; loss of job or loss of perspective? Whether that loss is temporary or permanent, you need to dig deep for courage to find hope in seemingly hopeless situations. In the face of frightening front page headlines, we must also remember that good and bad exists in all nations and denominations.

After 9/11, I had no idea that my poem 'Hope Happens!' would also become a book. If it helps even one person, I'll be happy.

● Catherine DeVrye, 'Hope Happens', in *Hope Happens: words of encouragement for tough times,* Everest Press, Australia, 2002.

OOO

KHOA DO

When he was two years old, Khoa left Vietnam on a fishing boat with his parents and forty other people. He has become a noted film director, writer and teacher in the Australian film industry. Khoa's latest film, *Footy Legends*, stars his brother, Anh Do. In 2005, Khoa was Young Australian of the Year.

> To love is to risk not being loved in return.
> To hope is to risk disappointment.
> But risks must be taken because the greatest risk in life is to risk nothing.
> The person who risks nothing, does nothing, sees nothing, has nothing and is nothing.
> He cannot learn, feel, change, grow, love and live.
>
> Author unknown

Reflections

For me, this passage means a lot. As I look back on my life, the most joyous times are those when I've taken the greatest risks.

And sure, often things don't quite work out. There are times when you fail, sometimes miserably. But when you make that decision and you take that risk – and put yourself, your hopes, and your vision out there for all the world to see – then you are truly living life.

I believe we have to make the most of our lives. I believe we should enjoy the time we have here, not take ourselves too seriously, and follow our dreams.

OOO

PETER DOHERTY, AC

In 1996 Peter and his Swiss colleague, Rolf Zinkernagel, were awarded the Nobel Prize in Medicine for their discovery of how the immune system recognises virus-infected cells. He divides his time between a research hospital in the United States and the University of Melbourne in Victoria. Peter was Australian of the Year in 1997.

> The ant's a centaur in his dragon world.
> Pull down thy vanity, it is not man
> Made courage, or made order, or made grace,
> Pull down thy vanity, I say pull down.
> Learn of the green world what can be thy place
> In scaled invention or true artistry,
> Pull down thy vanity,
> Paquin pull down!
> The green casque has outdone your elegance.
>
> Ezra Pound

Reflections

What these powerful lines say to me is that we must cease to stand apart from nature, we must master ourselves and our behaviour if we are to preserve the beauty of 'the green world' that is our place.

A fervent hope is that those who guide the great religions will re-think and interpret their diverse belief systems in ways that promote the wellbeing of the natural world. Setting aside cataclysmic natural events – the 'Acts of God' like earthquakes and tsunamis – our species Homo sapiens hold the health of all complex life forms in trust. Every ocean that is fished out, every acre that is transformed from arable land to desert and every species that is lost forever as a consequence of human over-population is a profound condemnation of us and of those who seek to guide our values and behaviour.

The great ethical, moral, political and technological challenge to those who currently inhabit this small planet is to develop sustainable systems that will ensure good, fulfilling lives for future generations. We have to deal with contemporary realities, and cannot be held hostage by practices appropriate for primitive agricultural communities in existence when the earth supported ten times fewer people. Look at the Middle East, where the Abrahamic religions developed, and ask, what has become of the fertile crescent?

Whether you believe in the primacy of God, of natural selection, or of something in between, it is clearly our responsibility to protect and maintain the viability, wonder and diversity of this miraculous creation. To do anything less is a profound betrayal of those who come after us. As the natural world thrives, so does the human spirit.

● Excerpt from Ezra Pound, 'Cantos 81', in *The Cantos of Ezra Pound: revised collected edition*, Faber & Faber Ltd, London, 1975.

Ezra Pound (1885–1972) was an American expatriate, poet, musician, critic and economist.

○○○

KEN DONE, AM

A contemporary Australian artist and designer, Ken left school when he was fourteen years old to enter the National Art School in east Sydney. After studying for five years, he commenced a highly successful career in New York, London and Sydney. Ken worked on the opening and closing ceremonies of the 2000 Olympic Games in Sydney.

> Look to this day. Yesterday is already a dream and tomorrow is only a vision. But today, well lived makes every day a dream of happiness and every tomorrow a vision of hope.
>
> **Sanskrit proverb**

Reflections

My father, Cliff Done, lived by this saying.

○○○

STEPHANIE DOWRICK

While living in London for many years, New Zealand-born Stephanie Dowrick founded a prestigious independent publishing house, The Women's Press. As author, her bestsellers include *Intimacy and Solitude; Forgiveness and Other Acts of Love; The Universal Heart* and *Choosing Happiness*. She was ordained as an Inter-faith minister in 2005.

May the blessings of God rest upon you.
May God's peace abide with you.
May God's presence illuminate your heart.
Now and forever more.

Hazrat Inayat Khan

Reflections

This Sufi blessing is a favourite of mine, primarily because of the power of the blessing itself, but also because the inspirational teachings of Hazrat Inayat Khan give a true understanding of what unites people beyond religious differences. This prayer was written on a card for me by my dearest friend when I set off for my ordination as an Inter-faith minister in New York in June 2005, and then, synchronistically, was also the blessing we used and gave in that service.

O Lord, remember not only the men and women of good will, but also those of ill will.
But do not remember all the suffering they have inflicted on us; remember the fruits we have bought, thanks to this suffering – our comradeship, our loyalty, our humility, our courage, our generosity, the greatness of heart which has grown out of all this.
And when they come to judgement let all the fruits which we have borne be their forgiveness.

Jewish Prayer. Author unknown

Reflections

When I was researching the subject forgiveness for my book *Forgiveness and Other Acts of Love*, I came across this extraordinary Jewish prayer – which is also a profound teaching on forgiveness – written by an unknown prisoner in Ravensbruck concentration camp. As the Jewish faith so often beautifully combines awe and intimacy, I use many of their prayers in my teaching and my private prayer life.

● Hazrat Inayat Khan (1882–1927) was founder of the Sufi Order International.

OOO

HEATH DUCKER

The extraordinary story of Heath's childhood adversity and success was featured on ABC's *Australian Story* in 2006. As the second eldest of ten children, Heath's family struggled as he was growing up, and he faced many challenges. Heath is now a lawyer and patron of Butterflies of Hope, a remembrance day dedicated to all child war victims.

Peace ...

Does not mean to be in a place
Where there is no noise, trouble or hard work
It means to be in the midst of all these things and still be calm in your heart.

Anonymous

Reflections

We live in an often turbulent world and can be torn from our truest self by pressures that abound. But the important aim of life should be to find peace within – from peace within comes peace that flows out – and this can change the world.

PROFESSOR
DEXTER DUNPHY, AM

Dexter has been the distinguished professor at the University of Technology, Sydney – since 2000. He is interested in the management of organisational change, human resource management and corporate sustainability, and he has many publishing credits in these areas.

> For whoever has not known himself has known nothing, but whosoever has known himself has simultaneously achieved knowledge about the depth of all things.
>
> Book of Thomas the Contender

Reflections

Life is a spiritual journey towards ever greater awareness of ourselves and our unity with this mysterious universe. The great spiritual teachers ask us to take the path of self-discovery and to engage in life with the fullness of our being. As I take this path, I discover that every day becomes an opportunity to learn and grow; I encounter other pilgrims along the way; we break bread together and share the meaning of our experiences in a celebration of life.

Excerpt from 'Book of Thomas the Contender' in *Nag Hammadi Library*, as quoted in Elaine Pagels, *The Gnostic Gospels*, Penguin Books, 1990.
Elaine Pagels is an American writer, professor, feminist and biblical scholar.

◯◯◯

JOHN EALES, AM

During his exemplary rugby union career, John led the Australian Wallabies to many wins, including two successful World Cup campaigns. John participated in eighty-six tests, fifty-five of them as Wallabies captain. He is now a leader in the corporate world.

A bird flew by this morning.
It was a wedge-tailed eagle.
Dad taught me that.
In fact, in my early years he taught me just about
everything I knew.

A bird flew by at lunchtime
But I didn't notice it.
Dad would have seen it.
We seek beauty and wonder far and wide yet we don't
see it in front of our eyes.
Dad always did.
He taught me that ...
... when I was finally prepared to listen.

A bird flew by this evening.
I didn't know what it was.
Dad would have known.
I wish he was here.
There is so much more I should have learnt.
There is so much more I need to know.

But with all I don't know
And all I didn't learn
I did learn one thing I will never forget.
I learnt there are birds that fly in the sky
And now I know there is one more angel

At home soaring with them...
Watching over us.

Keep teaching me, Dad
I am here to learn.

John Eales

Reflections

I wrote this poem, 'Lessons From My Teacher', when I was preparing the eulogy for my father's funeral. I had never written a poem before but it helped me through a sad time.

● John Eales, *Lessons from my Teacher*.

○○○

JOE EL-KHOURY

At four years old Joe came to Australia after his father died in Lebanon's civil war. He is currently a director of pastoral services and religious education at St Aloysius' College, Sydney. In 2004, he won a National Excellence in Teaching Award. Joe has worked as a volunteer companion for Camp Quality for over a decade.

You want to know me? You want to see my face?
I do not age with time; I do not fit into a space
I transcend the capacity of your eye, so who am I?
It is the question of the moment;
It is the question for all time
I am you, and you are mine

I am the beginning in the end
I am the faith in your believing
I am the color of truth
I am the dreamer of your dreams
I am the falling in your love
I am the words of a prayer
I am the silence in the music
I am the music in the silence

I am your father, I am your mother
I am the man who cannot cry
I am the story in your eyes
I am the orphan of war
I am the leper begging on the corner
I am the black slave in chains
I am the Muslim bride who cannot show her face
I'm the cross you carry again

I'm all you have forgotten
I am all that you have not been
I am in you – all of this is within you
Let the journey begin, Amen.
I am in you, Amen.

Danielle Rose

Reflections

This is a wonderful prayer/song as it reminds me to appreciate that God speaks to us through the small things in our life. He speaks to us in the beauty of nature and in the daily experiences and events of our lives, in the people we meet and what they say to us, or in what their presence asks of us.

Lyrics from Danielle Rose, 'God is', from the CD, *Defined Beauty* © J.S. Paluch Company Inc.

Danielle is an American singer/songwriter and Catholic music missionary who travels to schools, churches, conferences and retreats to share the music that she writes about Jesus. As a volunteer with Mother Teresa's Missionary Sisters of Charity, Danielle was given a rose by Mother Teresa to serve as a reminder to share her great gift that will unfold as a rose does, in God's time. She commemorates that in her professional name.

OOO

LIZ ELLIS

In 2005 Liz Ellis became the most capped Australian netballer of all time. Captain of the Australian team and the Sydney Swifts, Liz has an arts/law degree and is on the boards of various organisations, including the New South Wales Institute of Sport and the Sydney Olympic Park Sports Centre.

> ... only those who risk going too far can possibly find out how far one can go.
>
> **Attributed to TS Eliot**

Reflections

Throughout my sporting career I have come across some really inspirational and interesting quotations. This one appeals to me and has stayed with me because it is something instructional I can keep in mind when I am making decisions, training for netball or simply going about my day-to-day business.

To me it means that I shouldn't be constrained by what I or anyone else thinks I am capable of. You don't know how much you are capable of achieving until you push yourself. You can only find your limits by pushing yourself to go past them!

This saying also gives me comfort when I have 'gone too far' professionally or personally, and it reminds me that rather than the experience being a negative one, it is one that I can learn from.

● TS Eliot (1888–1965) was a US-born, naturalised British literary critic, dramatist and poet.

OOO

KATE ENGLEBRECHT

Kate is the director of Mission Possible Education, which seeks new ways to think about our mission. She has been involved in mission leadership in education and in health, and is editor of the book *Why I am Still a Catholic*, a collection of stories of faith and belief.

When I landed in the republic of conscience
it was so noiseless when the engines stopped
I could hear a curlew high above the runway.

At immigration, the clerk was an old man
who produced a wallet from his homespun coat
and showed me a photograph of my grandfather.

The woman in customs asked me to declare
the words of our traditional cures and charms
to heal dumbness and avert the evil eye.

No porters. No interpreter. No taxi.
You carried your own burden and very soon
your symptoms of creeping privilege disappeared.

Seamus Heaney

Reflections

I love this poem. It confronts me with the challenge of what authentic Christian discipleship really is all about. I particularly love the line: 'No porters. No interpreter. No taxi.'

This is how it feels sometimes when we choose to follow Jesus.

Excerpt from Seamus Heaney, 'Part 1' of 'The Republic of Conscience', in *Opened Ground Poems 1966–1996*, Faber & Faber Ltd, London, 1998.
Seamus Heaney (1939–) is an Irish poet and critic who won the Nobel Prize for Literature in 1995.

OOO

HAYLEY EVES

In 2001, at the age of fifteen, South-Korean-born Hayley represented Australian youth at the Centenary of Federation celebrations. She has a Bachelor of Business, majoring in Hotel Management and is currently completing a Graduate Management Traineeship.

Let there be peace on earth
And let it begin with me;
Let there be peace on earth,
The peace that was meant to be.

With God as our Father
Brothers all are we,
Let me walk with my brother
In perfect harmony.

Let peace begin with me,
Let this be the moment now;
With every step I take,
Let this be my solemn vow:

To take each moment and live each moment
In peace eternally.
Let there be peace on earth
And let it begin with me.

Jill Jackson

Reflections

I believe that we should all get on together and accept each other's differences and respect each other's ideas throughout the world, and be inclusive of everybody. I also believe if we each thought that change begins with ourselves, peace on earth could be achieved. I originally heard this song when I was in high school, at Christmas time, and its message has stayed with me since.

● 'Let There be Peace on Earth', lyrics by Jill Jackson and music by Sy Miller ©1955, renewed 1983, by Jan-Lee Music (ASCAP). International copyright secured. Reprinted by permission of Fable Music Pty Ltd (Australia).

This peace song has been sung in many countries and won numerous awards, including a Brotherhood Award from the National Conference of Christians and Jews.

PATTY FAWKNER

Patty has been a sister of the Good Samaritans for more than thirty years. Her studies have been in education, theology and pastoral ministry. Patty was a director of Uniya, the Jesuit Social Justice Centre, and is a member of the Council of Australian Catholic Women. Patty is also on the leadership team of her congregation.

The Mercy of God

I am copying down in a book from my heart's archives
the day that I ceased to fear God with a shadowy fear.
Would you name it the day that I measured my column
of virtue
and sighted through windows of merit a crown that was near?
Ah, no, it was rather the day I began to see truly
that I came forth from nothing and ever toward nothing-ness
tend,
that the works of my hands are a foolishness wrought in the
presence
of the worthiest king in a kingdom that never shall end.
I rose up from the acres of self that I tended with passion and
defended with flurries of pride;
I walked out of myself and went into the woods of
God's mercy,
and here I abide.
There is a greenness and calmness and coolness, a soft leafy
covering
from the judgment of sun overhead,
and the hush of His peace, and the moss of His mercy
to tread.
I have naught but my will seeking God; even love burning in
me
is a fragment of infinite loving and never my own.
And I fear God no more; I go forward to wander forever in a
wilderness made of His infinite mercy alone.

Jessica Powers

Reflections

Jessica Powers (1905–88) was an American Carmelite nun who 'tasted' – experienced – God's mercy as I have. The image of God she portrays is the God I want to love and worship and know. Jessica rejects a harsh-judging God – an image that dangerously lurks in my subconscious. God is mercy. God is love.

● Jessica Powers, 'The Mercy of God', in *The Selected Poetry of Jessica Powers*, ICS Publications, Washington DC, 1999. All copyrights Carmelite Monastery, Pewankee, WI. Used with permission.

○○○

ANTHONY FIELD

A member of The Wiggles, Anthony grew up in Sydney with six siblings and many cousins. There was always music in the Field household, and Anthony and his brothers played the music at mass while his mum played the organ.

When, like the rising day,
Love sends His early ray,
What makes His dawning glow
Changeless through joy or woe?
Only the constant know –

Youth must with time decay
Beauty must fade away,
Castles are sacked in war,
Chieftains are scattered far,
Truth is a fixèd star ...

Gerald Griffin

Reflections

I chose this song, 'Eileen Arun', because of the beautiful, thought-provoking lyrics, and because it's Irish!

● Gerald Griffin, 'Eileen Arun'.
    Gerald Griffin (1803–40) was an Irish novelist, lauded for his portrayals of Irish life, and especially the peasantry.
    Anthony also chose Psalm 23 (see page 19).

TIM FISCHER, AC

Tim's service in the Vietnam War gave him a lifelong identification with the Australian armed forces as well as an affinity with Asia. The former leader of the National Party of Australia, Deputy Prime Minister and Minister for Trade, has returned to farming, is a company director and is involved in charity work.

In the beginning was the Word, and the Word was with God, and the Word was God.

The same was in the beginning with God.

All things were made by him; and without him was not any thing made that was made.

In him was life; and the life was the light of men.

And the light shineth in darkness; and the darkness comprehended it not.

There was a man sent from God, whose name was John.

The same came for a witness, to bear witness of the Light, that all men through him might believe.

He was not that Light, but was sent to bear witness of that Light.

That was the true Light, which lighteth every man that cometh into the world.

He was in the world, and the world was made by him, and the world knew him not.

He came unto his own, and his own received him not.

But as many as received him, to them gave he power to become the sons of God, even to them that believe on his name:

Which were born, not of blood, nor of the will of the flesh, nor of the will of man, but of God.

And the Word was made flesh, and dwelt among us, (and we beheld his glory, the glory as of the only begotten of the Father), full of grace and truth.

John bare witness of him, and cried, saying, This was he of whom I spake, he that cometh after me is preferred before me; for he was before me.

continued overleaf

And of his fulness have all we received, and grace for grace.

For the law was given by Moses, but grace and truth came by Jesus Christ.

No man hath seen God at any time; the only begotten Son, which is in the bosom of the Father, he hath declared him.

John 1:1–18 King James Bible

Reflections

A back-to-basics text that reminds us all that there was a beginning and that was with God and that was God, and by dint of all of this, evil will be overcome. At dawn or even sunset, just ahead of a rising full moon, it is great to take a walk to meditate and reflect on the beginning and all that it means, and so enjoy communicating with the overarching masterful one.

I do not dwell on all of this as I prefer privacy with my not-frequent-enough prayers, but I commend this section of the Bible as a guiding fundamental truth.

OOO

KING FONG, OAM

An importer of Chinese groceries, King Fong has spent many years in volunteer welfare support, public relations and education. He has held executive positions with organisations like the Young Chinese Relief Movement, New South Wales Chinese Chamber of Commerce and the Australian Chinese Community Association. King was ambassador for Seniors Week in 2005.

One, two, three
What can I see?
Your future's looking bright,
It is time that we belong
to the mainstream heights.

So let's share the spirit,
Let us strengthen our aims,
Time will help us to survive
And we'll make some gains ...
Soon you'll see,
that it's a chance
to go on and dance ...
Many opportunities
will come along your way,
This will make you want to stay
In our land of hope ...

So, let's share the spirit,
Let us strengthen our aims,
Time will help us to survive
And we'll make more gains ...

King Fong

Reflections

These lines, written and composed through personal experience, are a constant reminder of the joy of gaining such experiences in the welfare and social community.

King Fong, 'Time to Rejoice', presented at the Sydney Chinese Community Committee Support 'Sydney Olympic 2000 Bid', 1993.

JACKIE FRENCH

A full-time author with more than 130 books published over seventeen years, Jackie writes fiction and non-fiction for children and adults and has regular columns in print media. Her books have won many awards, particularly *Hitler's Daughter* and *Diary of a Wombat*. Jackie is a keen gardener and wombat lover.

Let me see life like a wombat: To always be conscious of the past and the future, not just the 'now'; to rejoice in the feel of the air on my skin, the taste of the wind and the smell of the soil and the sky; to find as much joy in the softness of my bed and the taste of my breakfast as any larger achievement; to surround myself with the things that make me human – friends and family and kind society, animals and birds and the myriad species of the earth; and like a human (not a wombat) to praise and give thanks in everything that I do, with fullness of heart, always.

Jackie French

Reflections

A wombat 'sees' with its sense of smell, so it experiences the past as well as the present, with a hint perhaps of the future. Sometimes I think that humans forget that we are part of the natural world, not just its modifier; and if we forget the natural heart of our world, we lose our humanity, too.

HARRY GALLAGHER, OAM

As an eighty-three year old, Harry is still unstoppable. Throughout his career he has coached many Australian Olympic swimmers, including Dawn Fraser. Between Harry's pupils, nine Olympic gold medals have been won and fifty-seven world records have been broken. He is the author of five books and currently manages a squad of 180 swimmers.

Every day I need you, Lord.
But these days especially I need some extra strength
to face whatever is to be.
These are the days I need to feel you near,
to fortify my courage, to overcome my fear.
For by myself I cannot meet my challenge
of the hour.

Anonymous

Reflections

In 1994 I was at a low point, in hospital with cancer. The chemotherapy almost killed me. Sister said, 'We lost you for a while', but I survived, and so did my faith. This inspirational prayer I know helped me.

● These words are from an inspirational card that was in the cancer ward at Royal Prince Alfred Hospital, Sydney.

RICHARD GILL, OAM

Richard is a conductor and world-renowned music educator. He regularly conducts for Opera Australia, the major Australian orchestras and the state opera companies. Richard has received numerous awards, most recently the Australia Council Don Banks Award in 2006.

Make a joyful noise unto the Lord, all ye lands.
Serve the Lord with gladness:
come before his presence with singing.
Know ye that the Lord he is God:
it is he that hath made us, and not we ourselves
we are his people, and the sheep of his pasture.
Enter into his gates with thanksgiving,
and into his courts with praise:
be thankful unto him, and bless his name.
For the Lord is good;
his mercy is everlasting;
and his truth endureth to all generations.

Psalm 100 King James Bible

Reflections

The idea of a joyful noise being made to the Lord allows all mankind to make music and praise in any way, as long as it's joyful; no talent is required other than the talent the Lord gave you, and He is a God of song.

● Richard also chose the 'Prayer of St Francis' (see page 43), and 'The Serenity Prayer' (see page 154).

○○○

RUBY LANGFORD GINIBI

An eminent Aboriginal author, lecturer and historian, Ruby was born on Box Ridge Aboriginal mission in New South Wales and attended Casino High School until second form – her only formal education. Her books, including the groundbreaking memoir *Don't Take Your Love to Town*, have brought Aboriginal experiences to new audiences.

In this room I have all my personal photographs. Mum and Dad's photo hangs above my head. I talk to them when I am lonely, I say 'Marmi and Marman[1] look after me when I am asleep'. Then inside the door is my daughter Pearl's Big Photo. She made history in 1968 being the first ever Aboriginal to dance with a prime minister (John Gorton). I lost Pearl and my eldest son Bill in 1969 and 1970 – only eight months between their deaths. I call out to them – '"My Pepe" I called Pearl, and "William Henry" nynars jarjums[2] I love youse and miss youse. Stay with me and watch over me tonight nynars jarjums.'

On the other wall near my TV is a photo of my four sons: Nobby with Jeff on his knees and David next to him, then my Bill. Under this photo is one of my daughter Aileen's two children, Stella and Mathew; also my first great-granddaughter, McKalya Jade, a coupla' months old cuddling big Pumpkin (my daughter Pauline's granddaughter).

Further along the same wall is my grandson. I looked after him when he was born, while my Ellen worked as pink lady bringing the meals round at the Royal Prince Alfred Hospital. The photos of my son Nobby were taken in Long Bay prison. Next a photo of my two full sisters Gwen and Rita. They are my titas[3] and I talk to them also, cause I don't see much of them now; this photo was taken 22 years after we left our little home town of Bonalbo in New South Wales. Then right in the corner is a photo of

continued overleaf

me taken at a police ball at Sydney Town Hall in 1953 when I was 18 and had my two eldest children. When I look at this photo of me, I'm quite taken aback, cause I don't know where this goodlookin' woman went to! It certainly doesn't look like me now! Cause BK (before kids) I had a 22-inch waist, 34-inch bust and hips. Wow! That was a Real deadly age, now I'm 50, 60 and 70. Ha ha. You have ta laugh. There is a big framed photo with all my grandchildren at various stages of their childhood. Most of them have gone their own way in life and have children of their own. And life goes on. Doesn't it!

Before I nod off to sleep every night I call out to the good spirit Cooradji or Birrigan Gargli or Nundjigalli or Biame[4] the Great Spirit, he has many names in our Bundjalung culture. And I ask him to look after all my jarjums and grandjarjums[5] and nynars great grandjarjums of this land, because they are our future generations.

Ruby Langford Ginibi

[1] mum and dad; [2] my children; [3] sisters; [4] the sky deity (God) or our good and great spirit in heaven; [5] grandchildren

 Ruby also chose Psalm 23 (see page 19) as she loved it at Sunday School.

○○○

KATHERINE GOODE

A member of the Adelaide Jewish community, Katherine has worked as a teacher, journalist, playwright and children's writer. Currently she is the coordinator of Project Abraham, a federally funded multi-faith program in Adelaide.

Words there are and prayers, but justice there is not, not yet peace.

The prophet said: In the end of days God shall judge between the nations: they shall beat their swords into plowshares and their spears into pruninghooks.

Although we must wait for judgment, we may not wait for peace to fall like rain upon us.

The teacher said: Those who have made peace in their house, is as though they have brought peace to all Israel, indeed to all the world.

Peace will remain a distant vision until we do the work of peace ourselves. If peace is to be brought into the world, we must bring it first to our families and communities.

The psalmist said: Seek peace and pursue it.

Be not content to make peace only in your own household: go forth and work for peace wherever men and women are struggling in a cause.

Jewish Prayer

Reflections

I chose this meditation from our prayer book, *Gates of Repentance*, because it sums up the essence of our multi-faith program, Project Abraham, which is dedicated to creating a model for peace and reconciliation between Muslims, Christians and Jews.

The genesis for our federally funded program occurred one afternoon while my cousin from Israel and I were strolling through Rundle Mall in Adelaide. My cousin stopped in front of the entrance to the new David Jones shopping complex. She glanced around furtively and said, 'There are no soldiers. There are no armed guards. There are no policemen.' Then she sighed and shrugged. 'I guess I'm going to have to get used to this.'

At that moment, my heart broke and I vowed if there was something I could do, some small gesture to bring peace to this troubled world, I would do it. That promise has been realised in Project Abraham.

■ 'Seek Peace and Pursue it', in *Gates of Repentance: The New Union Prayer Book for the Days of Awe*, ©1979 Central Conference of American Rabbis and Union of Progressive Synagogues. Used with permission.

◯◯◯

DOCTOR
GERARD GUITON

A peace activist and educationist, Gerard has worked for international development agencies and is active in the Quaker movement. At present he is conducting historical and theological research. He is the author of *The Growth and Development of Quaker Testimony* (2005) and *Stillness* (1994).

Stand still in that which is pure, after ye see yourselves; and then mercy comes in. After thou seest thy thoughts, and the temptation, do not think, but submit, and then power comes. Stand still in that which shows and discovers, and then doth strength immediately come. And stand still in the Light, and submit to it, and the other will be hushed and gone; and then content comes.

George Fox

Reflections

Quaker prayer is a multivaried thing. We don't tend to pray to a God out there but *with* God; we tune in to a love dimension, so to speak. In our Meetings for Worship the ideal is, as Meister Eckhart (Christian mystic) says, 'to let go even of God' but recognising also that we are 'one of each other'.

For the early Quakers of the seventeenth century, prayer was no adjunct to the weekly round, still less the formulaic mantra of the church pew. Real prayer, to borrow the words of the medieval anchorite Julian of Norwich, was seen to 'oneth the soul with God' and to set in motion one's faith in hope and charity. Hence the Friends were exhorted to walk cheerfully with joy and courage over the earth, as priests sanctified by God. They were to do so without intermediaries such as creedal statements or church dogma, though the Bible provided the framework by which their beliefs and practices matured. The very immediacy of their dialogue with God meant Friends required themselves to 'wait upon', 'dwell in', 'stand still in', 'walk in', 'draw more and more into', and strive to be in the life and power of God's presence.

⬤ Excerpt from Epistle No. 10, in *The Works of George Fox*, Philadelphia: Gould, 1831, vol.1. p.20. George Fox (1624–91) was the principal founder of the Religious Society of Friends, the Quakers.

○○○

MAJOR
JOYCE HARMER, OAM

A trained nurse, Joyce was born in Gympie and married at twenty. The following year she began training as a Salvation Army officer. In her work as a Salvation Army court chaplain, Joyce gave non-judgmental support to those who 'had made the wrong choice in life' as well as to those affected by these decisions.

I am praying, blessed Saviour,
To be more and more like thee;
I am praying that thy Spirit
Like a dove may fall on me.

I am praying to be humbled
By the power of grace divine;
To be clothed upon with meekness
And to have no will but thine.

I am praying, blessed Saviour,
And my constant prayer shall be
For a perfect consecration
That shall make me more like thee.

continued overleaf

Thou who knowest all my weakness,
Thou who knowest all my care,
While I plead each precious promise,
Hear, O hear, and answer prayer.

Fanny Crosby

Reflections

Over the years the words of this hymn by Fanny Crosby have meant much to me in my spiritual life. It is a fact of spiritual living that no one 'spiritual aid', such as the hymn I have quoted, can be taken in isolation. When I sing the words of this hymn, as each verse progresses, I think of scripture to reinforce the words that I sing.

The first verse reminds me of Romans 12:1–2, where Paul exhorts believers to 'Present your bodies as a living sacrifice … be not conformed to this world, but be … transformed by the renewing of your mind'. The last line brings to mind an image of the baptism of our Lord as recorded in Mark 1:9–11.

The second verse reminds me of 2 Timothy 2: 1–2, where we are encouraged to 'Be strong in the grace that is in Christ Jesus', and also of the sermon on the Mount, where Jesus said, 'Blessed are the meek; for they shall inherit the earth' (Matthew 5:5).

The third verse reminds me that I should live in an 'atmosphere of prayer', as is written in Ephesians 6:18, and also that my dedication must keep pace with his revealed will for my life.

The chorus provides me with understanding that my heavenly Father knows my weaknesses. My life has not been without its trials, and many times I have felt keenly the frailty of how human I am, and at times the circumstances of life overwhelmed me – for this reason, the chorus is of such spiritual significance to me. In my morning devotions, I am reminded again and again of the scripture from Ephesians 2: 8–9: 'For by Grace are ye saved through faith; and that not of yourselves; it is the gift of God: not of works, lest any man should boast.'

I could not exist without my faith in Jesus Christ, and the knowledge that at all times I am surrounded by the blessed Holy Spirit as promised by Jesus in John 14:16: 'I will pray the Father, and he shall give you another Comforter, that he may abide with you for ever.'

● Excerpt from Fanny Crosby, 'I am Praying, Blessed Saviour'.
Fanny Crosby (1820–1915) was a blind American hymn-writer and poetess.
Joyce Harmer also chose the 'Prayer of St Francis' (see page 43).

DANI HASKI

Dani Haski worked for many years in theatre, film and television wardrobe departments before becoming a producer. Her *Australian Story* episode, 'Out of the Dust', on ABC Television, about a roadside memorial ceremony for her brother, was screened in September 2005 to broad acclaim.

We pause in reverence before the gift of self:
The vessel shatters, the divine spark shines through,
And our solitary self becomes a link
In Israel's golden chain.
For what we are, we are by sharing. And as we share
We move toward the light.

We pause in reverence before the mystery of presence:
The near and far reality of God.
Not union, but communion is our aim.
And we approach the mystery
With deeds. Words lead us to the edge of action.
But it is deeds that bring us closer to the God of light.

We pause in terror before the human deed:
The cloud of annihilation, the concentrations for death,
The cruelly casual way of each to each.
But in the stillness of this hour
We find our way from darkness into light.

May we find our life so precious
That we cannot but share it with the other,
That light may shine brighter than a thousand suns,
With the presence among us of the God of light.

Rosh Hashanah Meditation

Reflections

I found this meditation in the prayer book I use for the Jewish festivals of Rosh Hashanah (Jewish New Year) and Yom Kippur (the Day of Atonement). For me, these stanzas describe the essence of memorial – from internal self-reflection to sharing with community, then beyond, to a transcendent experience.

Tragedy, trauma and grief are transformative events, and far too many people in Australia are touched by the tragedy of road trauma. Recently my own childhood trauma has taken me on a life-changing journey. On a bright morning in August 1979, my ten-year-old brother, Ben, was on a school excursion in the outback when the vehicle he was travelling in collided head-on with a panel van on a red dirt road, halfway between Bourke and Brewarrina. Eight young people died, aged between ten and twenty-two years old.

In 2004, twenty-five years after this tragic accident, I organised a memorial ceremony by the side of that road, and the families met, many for the first time. We stood and remembered our loved ones and shared our feelings.

Trauma and grief have form and mass that we carry inside us. It slips and sloshes around inside our hearts, sometimes spilling out at inappropriate moments. With time, it is contained, and the load is more manageable. Talking about our loved ones and sharing our experience slowly transforms grief and reshapes the anguish. Memorials allow us to feel heard; for our pain to be validated; for our anguish to be acknowledged.

Much healing at our roadside memorial happened without words. It took place in looks and handshakes and embraces, which communicated eloquently our understanding and empathy with each other.

This is the power of memorial: the comfort offered by sharing as part of a community, the strength that comes from being a link in a chain connecting one to the other, and the light which lifts the darkness of despair.

● Excerpt from morning service for Rosh Hashanah, in *Gates of Repentance: The New Union Prayer Book for the Days of Awe*, ©1979 Central Conference of American Rabbis and Union of Progressive Synagogues. Used with permission.

OOO

ANNE HENDERSON

Anne was born in Melbourne and is the eldest of seven. A former secondary school teacher, she writes non-fiction books, including the biography of Joyce Harmer (see her entry on page 89), *An Angel in the Court: the life of Major Joyce Harmer*. Anne also works as the deputy director of the Sydney Institute.

Though the fig tree does not bud
and there are no grapes on the vine,
though the olive crop fails and the
fields produce no food,
though there are no sheep in the pen
and no cattle in the stalls,

Yet I will rejoice in the Lord,
I will be joyful in God my saviour.

The Sovereign Lord is my strength;
he makes my feet like the feet of a deer,
he enables me to go on the heights.

Habakkuk 3:17–19 New International Version Bible

Reflections

My sister, Mary, mother of a young daughter, died in 1988. She was thirty years old. Mary knew she was dying for many months, while often bedridden in a room where she surrounded herself with mementos of loved ones and words that kept her strong. Among her favourites were these lines of Habakkuk and they, in time, gave me the strength to accept the very sad way she had to go. It is a prayer for me that inspires hope in the face of despair – one particularly relevant for the times. Mary's family and friends read these lines during the requiem before we buried her, and I keep them with me always.

○○○

PHILLIP HINTON

Phillip began working in radio when he was fourteen years old. His career as an actor and voice artist spans over four decades in radio, stage, television and film. A member of the Bahá'í Faith since 1961, Phillip has spoken on behalf of the Bahá'í Faith in many countries.

I think continually of those who were truly great.
Who, from the womb, remembered the soul's history
Through corridors of light where the hours are suns,
Endless and singing. Whose lovely ambition
Was that their lips, still touched with fire,
Should tell of the Spirit, clothed from head to foot in song.
And who hoarded from the Spring branches
The desires falling across their bodies like blossoms.

What is precious, is never to forget
The essential delight of the blood drawn from ageless
springs
Breaking through rocks in worlds before our earth.
Never to deny its pleasure in the morning simple light
Nor its grave evening demand for love.
Never to allow gradually the traffic to smother
With noise and fog, the flowering of the Spirit.

Near the snow, near the sun, in the highest fields,
See how these names are fêted by the waving grass
And by the streamers of white cloud
And whispers of wind in the listening sky.
The names of those who in their lives fought for life,
Who wore at their hearts the fire's centre.
Born of the sun, they travelled a short while toward
the sun
And left the vivid air signed with their honour.

Stephen Spender

Reflections

I'm inspired by Spender's poem. It affirms my own belief as a Bahá'í that our fundamental nature is spiritual and that 'the flowering of the Spirit' (note the capital S!) demands conscious choices, patience, and fortitude under trials. The poet seems to say that 'true greatness' is not the sum of material achievements in our lives but the spiritual and moral courage we exert in remaining on 'the road less travelled'.

● Stephen Spender,'I think continually of those who were truly great' in *The Penguin Book of English Verse*, ed. John Hayward, Penguin Books, 1956. Published by Allen Lane, 1978.
Stephen Spender (1909–95) was an English poet and critic.

○○○

MELANIE HOGAN

In 2000, Melanie left her career in investment banking and started filmmaking. Her award-winning film *Kanyini*, the first documentary she produced and directed, screened in Australian cinemas in 2006. It features an Aboriginal man, Bob Randall (see his entry on page 149), who talks about how Indigenous people struggle in a modern world and explores ways to move forward.

> It is natural for human beings
> to live in harmony with each other.
>
> Tjilpi Wiriyanjara

Reflections

Deep in my heart I dream of a world where all humans can feel the beauty of being alive together.

● Tjilpi Wiriyanjara is a senior elder from the Pitjantjatjara lands, South Australia; a place where he was born and has resided in all of his life.

○○○

THE RIGHT REVEREND DOCTOR
PETER HOLLINGWORTH, AC, OBE

Peter worked at the Brotherhood of St Laurence for twenty-five years, ten years as executive director, has a Master of Arts in Social Work and has written several books. He was Archbishop of Brisbane 1990-2001, Australian of the Year in 1991 and was Governor-General of the Commonwealth of Australia from 2001 to 2003.

> O Lord, support us all the day long of this troublous life, until the shadows lengthen and the evening comes, the busy world is hushed, the fever of life is over and our work is done. Then, Lord, in thy mercy, grant us a safe lodging, a holy rest, and peace at the last.
>
> Attributed to John Henry Cardinal Newman

Reflections

Newman's reflection is a reflection on the end of each day and the end of our earthly life. I have always used this at funeral services and would like it at mine. Right now, however, the shadows have not yet lengthened and my work is not yet done.

● Used by Cardinal Newman (1801–90), but generally thought to be a sixteenth-century prayer.

OOO

GABI HOLLOWS

Gabi's interest in ophthalmology began when she had eye surgery as a toddler. During her orthoptic training she met Professor Fred Hollows. They worked together on the National Trachoma and Eye Health Program and later married. Gabi was a founding director of The Fred Hollows Foundation, and since Fred's death she has continued her involvement with this organisation.

In this pain and sadness which weighs me down and for which I can find no human support, I turn to you Saint Martin. Be my friend and my protector and intercede for me to our merciful Father in heaven. Ask that my sins be forgiven and that I may be freed from the evils which burden and distract me. Give me your spirit of sacrifice that I may welcome whatever God sends for love of him who makes all things a means of holiness.

Oh heavenly Father, in the name of your Son and of his blessed Mother, and by the merits of your faithful servant Martin, help me in my great trouble and do not forsake me!

Saint Martin de Porres Prayer

Reflections

This prayer has always been a focal point in my life. It reminds me of my father, Sam O'Sullivan, my family, and where I grew up, as our farm was called 'St Martins'. My father was educated by the Jesuits and was a highly religious man who was frequently extremely ill with rheumatic heart disease. He was close to his aunt, Sister Mary Raphael, a Dominican nun, who introduced him to this saint. He always carried this prayer in his wallet and prayed frequently to St Martin. According to family anecdote, I would have been named Martin, had I been a boy.

Being the youngest in the family, I knew about death and tragedy quite early in my life. Prayer is special to me but is also private; it takes on many forms. Being thankful is an important part of my prayer.

● St Martin (1579–1639) was the first black South American saint and is venerated as a patron saint of social justice and race relations. A Peruvian lay brother in the Dominican order, he was known by locals as 'Father of the Poor'. He was beatified by Pope Gregory XVI in 1837 and canonised by Pope John XXIII in 1962.

MARGARET HOLMES

A pacifist and activist, ninety-eight year old Margaret Holmes has always based her work on Christ's teachings. In 1960 she started a branch of the Women's International League for Peace and Freedom in her home, campaigning against the use of atomic weapons. Her six children are her proudest achievement.

Here, in a quiet and dusty room they lie,
Faded as crumbled stone or shifting sand,
Forlorn as ashes, shrivelled, scentless, dry –
Meadows and gardens running through my hand ...

In this brown husk a dale of hawthorn dreams;
A cedar in this narrow cell is thrust
That will drink deeply of a century's streams,
These lilies shall make summer on my dust.

Here in their safe and simple house of death,
Sealed in their shells a million roses leap;
Here I can blow a garden with my breath,
And in my hand a forest lies asleep.

Attributed to Muriel Stuart

Reflections

I chose this poem because I found deep inspiration in the thought that such tiny things as seeds contained such incredible potential; the contrast between their size and what they could do is so amazing in itself and so symbolic of human endeavours.

● Muriel Stuart, 'The Seed-Shop'.
   In the 1920s Muriel Stuart (1885–1967) wrote with immense courage and profundity on sexual politics, love and nature.

○○○

SILMA IHRAM

A Muslim convert of thirty years and a mother to six children, Silma is an advocate for the Muslim community and has helped pioneer Islamic schooling in Australia. She founded the Al Noori Muslim Primary School and the Noor al Houda Islamic College.

> Praise the name of thy Lord the Most High,
> Who hath created, and further, given order and proportion;
> Who measureth, then guideth;
> And Who bringeth out the (green and luscious) pasture,
> Then turneth it to russet stubble.
> By degrees shall We teach thee to declare (the Message)
>   so thou shalt not forget,
> Except as Allah wills: For He knoweth what is manifest
>   and what is hidden.
> And We shall ease thy way unto the state of ease.
> Therefore remind (men), for of use is the reminder.
> He will heed who feareth ...
>
> Qur'an 87:1–10

Reflections

This passage reminds me always that every aspect of my strength and weakness is designed by Allah, and there is guidance specifically for every one of us according to what we individually need; also that life and history go through cycles – of success, failure, wealth and poverty. The most important aspect of life though is to remember Allah always – for that brings us happiness.

● Excerpt from Qur'an 87:1, 3, 5, 8–10 translated by Muhammad Marmaduke Pickthall, 1930; and Qur'an 87:2, 4, 6–7 translated by Abdullah Yusuf Ali, 1934.

TERRI JANKE

Terri is a solicitor of Indigenous descent with family connections to Cairns, the Torres Strait Islands (Meriam) and Cape York Peninsula (Wuthathi). Her law firm, Terri Janke and Company, specialises in Indigenous cultural and intellectual property. Terri is also a public speaker and author of the novel *Butterfly Song* published by Penguin in 2005.

In this world, there are many things
Some we've had and some we're holding on to
We share the sun – on different days
We wait with silence 'til tomorrow comes.

Hearts speak out
Shouting louder joy
Hearts are speaking out to say the gentle things
Hearts speak out, when tomorrow comes
Hearts are speaking out
We rule the world ...

War is time and hate is half the reason
We too busy making too many movies
We share the sun – on different days
We wait with silence 'til tomorrow comes.

A heart will break
We still go on living
My heart hears the sound that you're calling ...

Hearts speak out
Shouting louder joy
Hearts are speaking out to say the gentle things
Hearts speak out, when tomorrow comes
Hearts are speaking out
We rule the world ...

Toni Janke

Reflections

I chose this passage because it is a song that makes me focus on the bigger picture, when the little things get me down. To me, it's about not being afraid to speak what's in your heart.

My sister writes the best reflective lyrics, and the music is beautiful. Her songs fill my heart and throughout my life have given me strength. I cry with absolute happiness when I really listen to the words of this song; it can be embarrassing playing it in the car because at the lights people look over and think I'm strange! Toni writes many songs and prayers all of which I find very inspirational.

Toni Janke, 'Hearts Speak Out', from the album, *Hearts Speak Out*, © Toni Janke Productions, Sydney, 1993. Toni Janke is a self-taught musician, singer and songwriter. She writes lots of songs and has written many prayers which are available on her website tonijanke.com

○○○

JANE JEFFES

Documentary filmmaker Jane Jeffes began her career in England. Her radio program *Something Understood*, airs each Sunday on BBC Radio 4; it examines questions about human life, spirituality and religion via speech, music, prose and poetry. Her documentary *Silma's School* (see Silma Ihram's entry on page 91) received a standing ovation at the 2005 Sydney Film Festival.

> To travel through that long landscape and back, back to the high mountain above the town of a thousand houses exposed to the sea and the wind. Back through that wild and empty land – who are you? who am I? – without knowing what to expect, when all the instruments have been destroyed by the wind ... when nothing else remains but to continue ...
>
> She would go on ahead to arrange everything. And then return for him. It would be so easy to confirm the freedom already gained ...
>
> Come, he would think, breathless in the wind. The land which happened inside us no one can take from us again, not even ourselves. But God, such a long journey ahead for you and me. Not a question of imagination but of faith.
>
> André Brink

Reflections

I love the poetry, enigma and mystery of these lines, which come from my favourite novel, *An Instant in the Wind*.

Shortlisted for the 1976 Booker Prize, it is a powerful story of love, identity and survival: the story of a white European woman and a black slave set against the harsh landscape of the unexplored interior of eighteenth-century South Africa. After her explorer husband dies and his team flees, Elisabeth must rely on Adam, a runaway slave. As they make their way back across the unmapped wilderness towards the apartheid civilisation of Cape Town, their relationship evolves.

Years ago I produced a reading of this novel for BBC Radio 4. The final lines were later part of the inspiration for the BBC radio program *Something Understood* and bind me to many special people in my life. This passage taps into my own experience moving to Sydney – and might even provide an interesting inscription for my grave!

These lines speak to me about our own personal journey, the fragility of human relations and the relationships which give life meaning and hope, the enduring reality of moments of deep connection and the commitment and hope we can find in these connections. Against the harsh backdrop of the South African interior and an unseen backdrop of wide social prejudice, there is also a brave hope for our new world, as we struggle to overcome 'otherness', racism and prejudice now. Perhaps, in the end, a successful multicultural society is 'not a question of imagination but of faith'.

● Excerpt from André Brink, *An Instant in the Wind*, Vintage, London, 2000. Reprinted by permission of the Random House Group Ltd.
André Brink (1935–) is a South African-born novelist.

SAM JEFFRIES

Sam is a proud Murrawari man, born and raised in Brewarrina, western New South Wales. He chairs the Murdi Paaki Regional Assembly and the National Aboriginal Sports Corporation Australia, is a board member of the Western Catchment Management Authority and panel member of the New South Wales Aboriginal Trust Fund Repayment Scheme.

> My feeling about Aboriginal regional and community governance in the Murdi Paaki region is that it will get bigger and bigger until it reaches all the people. One day it will have its name on a placard saying that it is the vehicle that helped free its people from the chains of poverty and oppression.
>
> Sam Jeffries

Reflections

This is what I believe – it's visionary, but it's my own very strong internal belief.

I also like the way Bob Marley puts things in 'Redemption Song'. He urges people to free themselves from mental slavery. I believe people spend too much of their time in mental slavery, whether intentionally or unintentionally.

● The Murdi Paaki region, in western New South Wales, covers traditional lands of a number of Aboriginal nations, or language groups, including the Paakantji, Ngiyampaa, Wangaaybuwan, Ngemba, Wayilwan, Murrawari, Wangkumara, Muti Muti, Ualroi, Baranbinja, Malyangapa and Gamilaroi nations.

CAROLINE JONES, AO

One of Australia's most respected broadcasters and communicators, Caroline has been a film, radio and television writer, producer, director and reporter since 1963. She has written many books, most notably *An Authentic Life: finding meaning and spirituality in everyday life*. Caroline presents *Australian Story* on ABC Television.

> I will lift up mine eyes unto the hills,
> from whence cometh my help.
> My help cometh from the Lord,
> which made heaven and earth.
>
> The Lord shall preserve thee from all evil:
> he shall preserve thy soul.
> The Lord shall preserve thy going out and thy coming in
> from this time forth, and even for evermore.
>
> Psalm 121:1–2,7–8 King James Bible

Reflections

Psalm 121 was introduced to me years ago, in a Seventh Day Adventist hospital. I awoke from an anaesthetic to find a handmade card at eye level on the bedside cabinet. There was a pen sketch of rolling hills with a cross on the highest, a promise of prayers for my recovery, and the first verse of Psalm 121. At the time, I did not think of myself as having any particular faith. I remember feeling very much alone. The only thing that seemed solid to me was my career.

Feeling that I should be capable of looking after myself, I had admitted myself to hospital unaccompanied, and had not asked anyone to visit me. I was not hostile to Christianity nor to religion in general, but it seemed irrelevant to me. My religion at the time was journalism! However, excellent nursing and kindness were being offered to me in a Christian hospital, and I was grateful for that. So the card was congruent with my situation and I could accept the truth of its message because it was being acted out in my life. Nothing could have been more helpful to me at that time, and I am indebted to the anonymous nurse or chaplain who cared for my neglected soul in such a thoughtful way. The card is preserved in my journal.

Remembering the comfort Psalm 121 had given me, I read this to my father every night of the eight weeks in hospital leading to his death. I think it brought him some solace.

Excerpt from Caroline Jones, *An Authentic Life: Finding meaning and spirituality in everyday life*, ABC Books, Sydney, 2005.

FATHER
ROSS JONES, SJ

An honours graduate in biochemistry, and foundation principal of Loyola College in Sydney's Mount Druitt, Father Ross is rector of St Aloysius' College. Twice a year he leads groups of senior students to the Philippines, where they live with, serve and learn from the poor and marginalised.

Take hold of me, Lord.
Accept this offering of freedom,
of memory, of mind,
of will; these things I cling to
and count as my own.
All are your gifts, Lord.
Now I return them.
They are yours;
do as you will.
Give me only your free gift of love,
in this you give all.

St Ignatius Loyola

Reflections

The 'Suscipe' ('Take, Lord, Receive') is the prayer that St Ignatius gives the retreatant at the end of 'The Spiritual Exercises' (a thirty-day retreat). It springs from a profound realisation that everything is a gift. In response, the one who prays it offers it all back to God – in freedom and for service. As a Jesuit myself, the prayer is an important part of my spirituality. But over the years I have discovered very similar prayers written by St Angela Merici (founder of the Ursuline Sisters), Charles or John Wesley (in a Methodist hymn), Blessed Charles de Foucauld (founder of the Little Company of Jesus) and even the Indian Hindu poet Rabindranath Tagore. Such a unity of theme, for me at least, hints at a universal truth.

● St Ignatius Loyola, 'Suscipe', translation by Daniel Madigan, SJ, Georgetown University, Washington DC.
St Ignatius Loyola (1491–1556) founded the Jesuit Order of priests and brothers.

ZALMAN KASTEL

The son of Hasidic rabbis, Zalman's first vocation was education in the Jewish community. Attuned to the striving for virtue common to people from every creed, he co-founded the Goodness and Kindness Campaign (now called Together for Humanity Foundation), whereby teams of Christians, Jews and Muslims work with school students to promote acceptance.

I declare that I forgive every person who angered me, or wronged me, against my body, against my money, against my honour or self-esteem, or anything of mine; regardless of whether it was against their will or wilfully, an accident or intentional, whether by speech or action. I ask you that no one be punished on my behalf. And that I too am forgiven and that I do not sin any more. You understand us, people, we earn our bread with our very souls, we are like dried grass, a decomposing flower, a passing shadow, a vanishing cloud, a blowing wind, flying dust and a fleeting dream.

Please, put peace, life, and grace upon us, between people in families, within communities, workplaces, and in Israel to find a lasting and just peace for all the inhabitants of the holy land.

I will praise you because you have uplifted me, I cried out to you and you healed me. For it is only one moment in your anger, a life time with your good will. And I had said, in my tranquillity, I will never falter. But of course it was you who had set my mountain strong. Then you hid your face; I was frantic. To you, God I cried out. You have transformed my lament into dancing.

Rabbi Zalman Kastel

Reflections

There is a Yiddish saying: a half truth is a complete lie. This montage of traditional Jewish prayers resonates strongly for me. Letting go of the grudges that threaten to swallow me is incredibly liberating.

More broadly as a society, we have managed to learn that bigotry is wrong. Unfortunately it has been replaced at times with a new 'righteous racism' – the idea that it is acceptable to talk in a hateful manner about social and ethnic groups based on some behaviour by some members of these groups.

There is often a lack of perspective about these groups, stemming from a lack of appreciation of the fuller truth about them and their beautiful even if imperfect humanity. In addition to various coercive measures to seek peace, justice and security, letting go of some grievances and appreciating the good in 'the other' is essential. The last paragraph of this passage gives me strength and perspective when things are 'not going to plan'.

● Excerpt from Rabbi Zalman Kastel, interpretations based on Psalm 30:2, 3, 6–8, 12 (ascribed to King David), in *The Siddur-Jewish Prayer Book*, ed. Rabbi Shneur Zalman of Liadi, Kehot Publications Society, New York, 1996.

OOO

JENNY KEE

A pioneer in Australian fashion design, Jenny Kee created unique knitwear and garments, based on Australia's natural environment and the silhouettes and textiles of traditional ethnic clothing. Jenny was born to a Cantonese father and an Italian Anglo-Saxon mother. Her spiritual quest draws on Asian religious philosophy and practice.

---

om vajrasattva samaya
manupalaya, vajrasattva denopa titha,
dido me bhava, suto kayo me bhava, supo kayo me bhava,
anurakto me bhava, sarva siddhi me prayatsa,
sarva karma su tsame, tsittam shriyam kuru hum,
ha ha ha ha ho, bhagavan
sarva tathagata, vajra mame muntsa,
vajra bhava maha samaya sattva ah hum phet

Tibetan mantra

Reflections

It's my life's work now to bring about purification, healing and transformation. The mantra, or prayer, that I say all the time is the 'Vajrasattva Mantra'. The essential meaning of this mantra is: 'O Vajrasattva! Through your power, may you bring about purification, healing and transformation.'

I say this mantra many times a day – it is like a crutch to me – it supports me and helps to purify my many negative actions and emotions.

Excerpt from Lama Zopa Rinpoche, '*The Power of the Remedy: Mantra Recitation*' ('Vajrasattva Mantra'), ©2001 Lama Zopa Rinpoche. Courtesy Lama Yeshe Wisdom Archive (LamaYeshe.com).
    'Vajrasattva Mantra' is an ancient Tibetan Buddhist mantra, the Hundred Syllable Mantra. Lama Zope Rinpoche (1946–) is the spiritual director of the Foundation for the Preservation of the Mahayana Tradition.

○○○

ZULEYHA KESKIN

Sydney-born Zuleyha, of Turkish heritage, is a wife and mother who combines those roles with work as a community pharmacist, vice-presidency of Affinity Intercultural Foundation, teaching and graduate study. For her masters degree, she is writing a thesis entitled 'Inter-faith Dialogue from a Muslim Perspective'.

> O God, put between me and errors a distance as great as that which you have put between East and West. O God, cleanse me of my errors as a white garment is cleansed of dirt.
>
> Prophet Muhammad

Reflections

This prayer was said by the Prophet Muhammad (peace be upon him), even though he was sinless. Muslims believe that all prophets were infallible. As a role model for Muslims, he used to say the prayer so that his followers could learn and recite it. Prayer was a fundamental part of the Prophet's life. Many of the prayers that he recited have been recorded and are still recited by Muslims today. He encouraged Muslims to personalise their prayers, but he also let his prayers be heard, for those who wanted to use them.

I like this prayer because it teaches us that we should strive to perfect our life as much as possible. The prayer acknowledges that, as humans, we will make errors but that we can 'cleanse' ourselves from these errors. It encourages us to 'do good' in every aspect of our life, whether it be by interacting with others, in our relationship with God or by contributing to society.

🖢 Excerpt from Imam Bukhari's compilation of *Hadith*, vol. 8, book 7, in M Fethullah Gulen, *Prophet Muhammad, The Infinite Light 2,* Truestar Ltd, London, 1996.
　　Imam Bukhari (194–256 AH, or 810–870 AD) was a highly regarded Sunni Islamic scholar who compiled the book *Sahih Al-Bukhari*, which many Muslims consider to be the most imortant book after the Qur'an.
　　Zuleyah also chose Qur'an 1:1–7, the Opening of the Qur'an (see page 156).

○○○

IAN KIERNAN, AO

Ian was founder and chairman of Clean Up Australia and Clean Up the World, a community-based organisation which inspires and works with Australians to conserve our environment. Ian has received numerous awards, including Australian of the Year in 1994 and the prestigious United Nations Environment Programme Sasakawa Environment Prize.

> **If your dreams don't frighten you, they are not big enough.**
>
> **Attributed to George Bernard Shaw**

Reflections

I have often set high goals and it is the fear of failure that has been a great motivation for me.

● George Bernard Shaw (1856–1950) was an Irish dramatist and literary critic.

OOO

PETREA KING

Since her unexpected recovery from leukaemia in 1984, Petrea has been counselling and conducting residential programs for people facing life's most significant challenges. She is the author of several books and CDs and is a regular guest on ABC Radio.

Great Spirit, make me an instrument of your peace.
Where there is hatred, let me sow love.
Where there is injury, pardon.
Where there is discord, unity.
Where there is doubt, faith.
Where there is error, truth.
Where there is despair, hope.
Where there is sadness, joy.
Where there is darkness, light.
O Great Spirit, grant that I may not so much seek to be consoled, as to console.
To be understood, as to understand.
To be loved, as to love.
It is in giving that we receive.
It is pardoning, that we are pardoned.
It is in dying that we are born to eternal life.

Attributed to St Francis of Assisi

Reflections

During my inner desolation, I hibernated in the cave outside of Assisi where St Francis had likewise retreated to wrestle with his own spiritual turbulence. This prayer, which is attributed to him, and his writings gave me great solace.

🔵 Petrea's made some personal adjustments to the Prayer of St Francis.

MICHAEL KIRBY, AC, CMG

Michael is a justice of the High Court of Australia. After being admitted to the New South Wales Bar, he was appointed to the Australian Conciliation and Arbitration Commission. The youngest man to become a federal judge, he was also president of the New South Wales Court of Appeal.

Reflections

To outsiders, the Anglican Church must sometimes seem a little quaint. It is as if it cannot make up its mind whether it is Catholic or Protestant. From the very beginning, it has been this way. It is a kind of compromise of a church – very English as one would expect. In the words of the preface to *The Book of Common Prayer:*

> It has been the wisdom of the Church of England ever since the first compiling of her Public Liturgy, to keep the mean between the two extremes, of too much stiffness in refusing, and of too much easiness in admitting any variation from it.

Somewhere between the bells and smells of Rome and the hand-waving hallelujahs of Protestant sects, the Anglican order of service offers a comforting space. At least, this is so for those who grow up with the majestic language of Cranmer's *Prayer Book.*

I was raised in Concord, in Sydney's western suburbs. Imagine my puzzlement, then, when I found that the martyred Archbishop Cranmer had something directly to say to me and my neighbourhood every Sunday. He did so in the second 'Collect for Peace' – a prayer said in the service of morning prayer:

> O God who are the author of peace and lover of concord in knowledge of whom standeth our eternal life, whose service is perfect freedom; Defend us thy humble servants in all assaults of our enemies that we, surely trusting in thy defence may not fear the power of any adversaries, through the might of Jesus Christ our Lord.
>
> Amen.

With God as lover of Concord, I knew that he was on my side. But how beautiful and peaceful the words are. Just ponder on the use of the word 'standeth'. Reflect on the 'assaults of our enemies'. Think awhile on 'trusting in thy defence'. It is a prayer to strengthen the faint-hearted. Or so it has always seemed to me.

In quiet nights in darkest Afghanistan, in busy days of tumult in the courts, alone, and in crowds, I have said this prayer to myself. It is such a reassurance.

When my mother was dying in hospital in Sydney, I said the prayer to her. She was not a specially religious person. But she was certainly spiritual. I know that the image of peace, love and concord were with her at the end. They were also with me and with our family. Life is but a journey, with ups and downs, joy and pain. But I will always be grateful for the comfort of *The Book of Common Prayer*. And especially for the 'Collect for Peace'. May that peace be with us all, always.

> Excerpt from *The Book of Common Prayer*, 1662, Cambridge University Press (Crown's Patentee), Cambridge, 1997.

◯◯◯

CHRISTOPHER KREMMER

Christopher Kremmer is one of Australia's most respected and popular writers of literary non-fiction. Born in Sydney, he was educated at the University of Canberra, and spent a decade in Asia working as a foreign correspondent. His books, including *The Carpet Wars*, *Bamboo Palace* and *Inhaling the Mahatma*, empathetically portray different cultures.

> Faith is the bird that feels the light,
> And sings when the dawn is still dark.
>
> Attributed to Rabindranath Tagore

Reflections

India's great poet captures both the beauty of creation and the heroic bravery of true faith, whether in a supreme being, or humanity's loftiest ambitions and ideals, or simply in ourselves.

> Rabindranath Tagore (1861–1941) was an Indian poet, playwright and essayist. In 1913, he won the Nobel Prize in Literature.

LUCILLA LEUNG

Lucilla is president of the Australian Chinese Community Association of New South Wales. A social scientist by training, she has many years' experience working in the corporate sector, in public affairs, training and development, international human resources, management and international joint ventures.

Thank Heaven, thank Earth and thank all Ancestors,
Love country, love family and love all friends.

With Love, with Hope and with unfailing Faith,
Thousand kilos of heavy loads amount to mere nothing.
Million miles of journey seem to be not so far.

Field of Heart and Land of Blessing work in unison.
One global family across the seas is always my wish;
Of One heart million of us forward we march,
Harmony, Peace and Prosperity appear in front of us.

Lucilla Leung

會長的話

先友　念重遠　力願步前
祖朋　信不不　努我舉眼
謝地　有不為　共是齊現
地家　望搬路　地家心和
謝天　有一里　福一一融
愛國　愛斤萬　田海眾祥
謝　有千百　心四萬瑞

Reflections

I write this as encouragement to all members and friends of the Australian Chinese Community Association, to serve the community with devotion, commitment and integrity – united in effort, mind and spirit.

🔘 Lucilla Leung, Australian Chinese Community Association president's message, Sydney, 2006.

TOM E LEWIS

An Indigenous actor, artist and musician, Tom was born at Ngukurr (Roper River) in south-eastern Arnhem Land. His real name is Bu/Ngarl, which means 'shark'. He played the lead role in *The Chant of Jimmy Blacksmith,* and he is the focus and co-writer of the short film *Yellow Fella,* the first Australian Indigenous documentary chosen for official selection at the Cannes Film Festival.

there's this kind of quietness, sweeping over the land,
there's this kind of quietness, sweeping over the land [...]
i remember the time when i used
to climb the hills with my grandfather
and he'd go 'see that limb on the tree ...
just a branch with a bend ...
you can see it ... there
if you cut that bit over there ...
and you carry it all the way down the
hill ... you have to try and break it in two
to make the boomerangs

'and the wood, carry this wood down the
hill, and spend two days shaping it
and scraping the wood to get a fine sound'
and he said, 'you see the point of this
boomerang, it could be for the traveller'
who's the traveller?

'the postman' oh ...
where did he go, that postman

he would travel right through this country,
taking messages to families, way across the
other side, where the sun goes down. And
then again when the moon rises. He would
take them. Sealed in his boomerangs.

what would he do with it? I told you he'd
take messages. In a little piece of stick, or

a hair off a baby

continued overleaf

where did they all go?

i said there's this strangeness coming on
this country. The songs and the stories are
all gone quiet. I said quiet

you hear the birds fly, you could hear the
boomerangs ... playing, as you danced [...]

and you'd sing to walk this country

In those seasons, you would sing and
you would walk and you would play and dance

and the church bells of the bush,
would fill up the whole land, for miles

i see my old man sitting
underneath the tree
wiry, his hands barely raises the tin
with water in it to drink, where have
all the young men gone, to hold his
boomerangs. who would walk the land.
To be the traveller, with the boomerang,
where have they gone

there's this kind of quietness
sweeping over this land

where time had no meaning

Tom E Lewis

Reflections

The laws of the West can be changed on paper but the laws of my people will
always be with us.

Excerpt from Tom E Lewis 'Boomerang', music and lyrics by Tom E Lewis, from the
CD *Sunshine After Rain*, Skinnyfish Music Pty Ltd, © 2005, Winnelle, NT, Australia.

FRANK LOWY, AC

Frank is a one-time refugee who became a multi-billionaire through the growth of Westfield Group, the company he co-founded in Sydney in 1960 and is now the largest retail property group in the world. He is executive chairman of Westfield, chairman of the Lowy Institute for International Policy in Sydney and also of the Football Federation of Australia.

> On Rosh Hashanah they are inscribed, and on Yom Kippur they are sealed: How many shall pass away and how many shall be born; who shall live and who shall die; who shall live out his allotted time and who shall depart before his time; who shall perish by water and who by fire; who by the sword, who by a wild beast; who by hunger and who by thirst; who by earthquake and who by pestilence; who by strangulation, and who by lapidation; who shall be at rest and who shall wander; who shall be tranquil and who shall be harassed; who shall enjoy well-being and who shall suffer tribulation; who shall be poor and who shall be rich; who shall be humbled and who shall be exalted.

Attributed to Rabbi Amnon

Reflections

As a child, I recall, standing next to my father in the synagogue in our small Hungarian town. It was Yom Kippur, the Jewish Day of Atonement. The Nazis were deporting Jews from surrounding villages, and fear gripped our community. Most religious Jews had come to synagogue on this special day to plead with God not to forsake them. During the chanting of the prayer 'Unesaneh Tokef' by the rabbi, it is the custom of pious and religious men to put their prayer shawls over their heads – so they can shut out the world and turn inwards.

I can still hear the rabbi intoning the words: 'Who shall live and who shall die … who by fire and who by water …'. My father drew me in under his shawl. He was squeezing my hand and sobbing. I could feel his anguish. Two years later he would be taken to Auschwitz, never to return.

⬤ Excerpt from the prayer 'Unesaneh Tokef', in *Rosh Hashanah Machzor*.
The prayer is attributed to Rabbi Amnon of Mainz, an eleventh-century German scholar, and is found in *The Machzor*, a special prayer book used on High Holidays.

DON MACLURCAN

As a ten-year-old, Don was presented with an academic award by the terminally ill Professor Fred Hollows. Later, the experience inspired him to run from Perth to Sydney to raise money for The Fred Hollows Foundation. Don is researching the impact of nanotechnology on health care in developing countries.

To laugh often and much
To win the respect of intelligent people
And the affection of children,
To earn the appreciation of honest critics
And endure the betrayal of false friends,
To appreciate beauty,
To find the best in others,
To leave the world a bit better,
Whether by a healthy child, a garden patch
Or a redeemed social condition,
To know even one life has breathed easier
Because you lived,
That is to have succeeded.

Attributed to Ralph Waldo Emerson

Reflections

I first read this verse in a transcript of the late Professor Fred Hollows' eulogy, delivered the day of my eleventh birthday. It touched me because of the simple yet great challenge it presents: little steps, open mind, less ego.

● Ralph Waldo Emerson (1803-82) was an American poet and essayist.

SISTER
TRISH MADIGAN, OP

A Dominican sister, Trish has been active in interfaith dialogue for over ten years. She is executive officer of the Commission for Ecumenism in Broken Bay Catholic Diocese. Trish was a member of the Australian delegation that participated in two recent international inter-faith dialogue conferences in the Asian region.

Rejoice in the Lord always; again I will say, Rejoice. Let your gentleness be known to everyone. The Lord is near. Do not worry about anything, but in everything by prayer and supplication with thanksgiving let your requests be made known to God. And the peace of God, which surpasses all understanding, will guard your hearts and your minds in Christ Jesus.

Finally, beloved, whatever is true, whatever is honourable, whatever is just, whatever is pure, whatever is pleasing, whatever is commendable, if there is any excellence and if there is anything worthy of praise, think about these things. Keep on doing the things that you have learned and received and heard and seen in me, and the God of peace will be with you.

Letter of Paul to the Philippians 4:4–9
New Revised Standard Version Bible

Reflections

This text begins with the word 'Rejoice', which seems to me an important and natural response as we come to a realisation of our spiritual connection with God. I like the balance in this text between the values of justice, graciousness, truth and the appreciation of excellence; also the exhortation to learning and receiving, and the promise of peace. I see it as a program for my life as a Christian. This was one of the scripture readings I chose for my final profession (life vows) as a Dominican sister and it was read during the ceremony by my twin sister, Helen.

HIS EMINENCE ARCHBISHOP
MOR MALATIUS MALKI MALKI

Syrian-born Archbishop Malki Malki graduated from the St Ephraim Syrian Orthodox Theological Seminary Damascus, from the Syrian Orthodox Theological Seminary in India, and from the Greek Orthodox Theological College in Athens. He was consecrated as archbishop in 2003.

O Lord, Lover of mankind, bend toward us with Your love, prove in us your grace, satisfy our hunger from Your richness, quench our thirst with the sweet fountain of Your delight, sprinkle our hearts, O our Lord, with the beauty of Your purity, inscribe in our souls the symbol of Your promises, enrich us with Your love, adorn our hearts with the love of our neighbour, shower us with Your affection, lift our minds to the great height of Your Godhead and make us worthy to meet You joyfully. Change us into the likeness of Your glory; make us splendid temples for Your dwelling. O merciful Lord, remove from the world all temptations, chastisements and rods of wrath and make Your peace and tranquillity prevail in the four quarters of the world. O You, Prince of peace, make us worthy of the good end meant for the men of peace.

Amen.

St John of Sedreh

Reflections

This is the urgent remedy for the current spiritual and social infirmity of the world.

⬤Excerpt from Patriarch St John of Sedreh, *Book of the Divine Liturgy*, Metropolitan Mar Athanasius Yeshue Samuel, New Jersey, USA, 1991.

○○○

AMANDA MARTIN

Amanda and her family own and run a farm in Winton, New South Wales, an area hit with ongoing drought and low grain prices. She helped set up Women of Winton. In 2006 WOW's pink ribbon day raised money for breast cancer screening trials in Tamworth and Armidale – the event brought the community closer together.

> Satisfy us in the morning
> with your steadfast love,
> that we may rejoice and be glad all our days.
>
> Psalm 90:14 English Standard Version Bible

Reflections

For me, the key to being happy is to know God. I see each human being as an image-bearer, created by a personal God to know him and to enjoy him forever.

The everyday act of giving is a reflection of the one who held nothing back when he gave his son Jesus Christ to lay down his life for others. In the light of this wondrous gift, I know my life is to be lived reflecting the same selfless attitude.

In the bush the act of giving can unite a community. It binds people to share a moment or a lifetime together. It is the creator of memories and personal histories. It enables ordinary people to achieve extraordinary feats. Rural people share a common farming heritage. They are uncomplaining and tough, hardworking and self-effacing. They stand together when things are black, when prices collapse and the rain doesn't fall – or falls too much. The spirit of the bush is a full-bodied and generous spirit that gives and gives and then gives some more.

It is the spirit of our country.

OOO

JESSE MARTIN

In 1999, eighteen-year-old Jesse Martin became the youngest person in history to circumnavigate the globe solo, non-stop and unassisted. He currently runs exploratory sail expeditions in Papua New Guinea aboard the thirty-eight-foot Polynesian catamaran *Imajica*. When not travelling, Jesse spends time writing and public speaking.

> He was proud of his brig, of the speed of his craft, which was reckoned the swiftest country vessel in those seas, and proud of what she represented.
> She represented ... long days of planning, of loving care in building; the great joy of his youth, the incomparable freedom of the seas; a perfect because a wandering home; his independence, his love – and his anxiety.
>
> Joseph Conrad

Reflections

No other passage I know of better describes the dream to me. It was shown to me by a very special person.

 Excerpt from Joseph Conrad, *The Rescue: a romance of the shallows*. First published in 1920.
Joseph Conrad (1857–1924) spent many years working in the French and British merchant navies before settling in Britain writing short stories and novels.

OOO

JESSIE MAULDER

Jessie is a twenty-two-year-old medical student, who was in Thailand during the tsunami of 2004. She became a volunteer in a makeshift morgue in the city of Krabi. Jessie hopes to use her medical degree to work in countries where health care is needed but not readily accessible.

> **If you are showing love to your fellow human beings, you are showing love to your God.**
>
> His Holiness the Dalai Lama

Reflections

This quote captures a very powerful aspect of humanity that we are all capable of expressing.

 Excerpt from His Holiness the Dalai Lama, *The Dalai Lama, Words of Wisdom: selected quotes from his Holiness the Dalai Lama*, compiled by Margaret Gee, Margaret Gee publishing, 1992.

His Holiness, Tenzin Gyatso (1935–), the fourteenth Dalai Lama, is the spiritual and temporal leader of the Tibetan people.

○○○

PROFESSOR
RON McCALLUM, AO

Blind since birth, Ron is professor of industrial law at Blake Dawson Waldron, dean of the Faculty of Law at the University of Sydney until October 2007, a board member of Vision Australia and chairs 2 RPH, radio for the print-handicapped. He finds calmness in music, meditation and quiet prayer.

And if tonight my soul may find her peace
in sleep, and sink in good oblivion,
and in the morning wake like a new-opened flower
then I have been dipped again in God, and new-created.

And if, as weeks go round, in the dark of the moon
my spirit darkens and goes out, and soft, strange gloom
pervades my movements and my thoughts and words
then I shall know that I am walking still
with God, we are close together now the moon's
in shadow.

And if, as autumn deepens and darkens
I feel the pain of falling leaves, and stems that break
in storms
and trouble and dissolution and distress
and then the softness of deep shadows folding, folding
around my soul and spirit, around my lips
so sweet, like a swoon, or more like the drowse of a low,
sad song
singing darker than the nightingale, on, on to the solstice
and the silence of short days, the silence of the year, the
shadow,

then I shall know that my life is moving still
with the dark earth, and drenched
with the deep oblivion of earth's lapse and renewal.

And if, in the changing phases of man's life
I fall in sickness and misery
my wrists seem broken and my heart seems dead
and strength is gone, and my life
is only the leavings of a life:

and still, among it all, snatches of lovely oblivion, and
snatches of renewal
odd, wintry flowers upon the withered stem, yet new,
strange flowers
such as my life has not brought forth before, new
blossoms of me –

then I must know that still
I am in the hands [of] the unknown God,
he is breaking me down to his own oblivion
to send me forth on a new morning, a new man.

DH Lawrence

Reflections

This is a poem that speaks of a life marked by struggle; and of a man who was ultimately at peace with his God.

● DH Lawrence, 'Shadows', in *The Faber Book of Religious Verse*, ed. Helen Gardner, Faber and Faber, London, 1972. Reproduced by permission of Pollinger Limited and The Estate of Frieda Lawrence Ravagli.
   David Herbert Lawrence (1885–1930) was an English novelist, poet and critic.

OOO

JEFF McMULLEN, AM

There has never been a line between Jeff McMullen's work as a journalist, author and filmmaker and his advocacy efforts. He is passionately committed to improving the education and health of Indigenous children, in Australia and overseas. Jeff is chief executive officer of Ian Thorpe's Fountain for youth.

> **Each day is a precious opportunity.**
> **Use every breath and you will make a difference.**
>
> Jeff McMullen

Reflections

With the late and great French vulcanologists Maurice and Katia Kraft, I climbed a volcano as it was blowing its top. 'Why worry?' said Maurice. 'In four-and-a-half billion years the earth will be engulfed by the sun and we will all be stardust.'

When you think of the great continuum, our petty fears and anxieties fade away. Even the most perilous challenges are no longer daunting when you remind yourself of the wonder, the sheer exhilaration of being alive. After seeing three dozen wars, I do not take life for granted. But I remember that the decency and commonsense of humankind has seen off Hitler, Stalin, Mao, Pol Pot and Idi Amin. The madmen of this hour will not prevail because the goodness of humanity will sweep them away.

○○○

LUKE McPHARLIN

Luke plays Australian Rules football for the Fremantle Football Club in Western Australia. In 2005, he was honoured to receive the Mark of the Year Award. Luke is currently studying pharmacy at Curtin University of Technology. He is also a singer-songwriter.

O Son of Being!

Thou art My lamp and My light is in thee.
Get thou from it thy radiance and seek none other than Me.
For I have created thee rich, and have bountifully shed My favour upon thee.

Bahá'u'lláh

Reflections

A favourite passage I put to music.

● Excerpt from Bahá'u'lláh, 'Part 1: from the Arabic', in *The Hidden Words of Bahá'u'lláh*, p. 6. © Bahá' World Centre, Haifa, Israel.

Bahá'is believe that Bahá'u'lláh is the messenger of God for this day. His teachings are the basis of the Bahá'i Faith, whose primary aim is the unity of mankind.

○○○

DOROTHY McRAE-McMAHON

A retired Uniting Church minister, Dorothy now volunteers with the parish in Redfern, Sydney. She writes liturgical material for churches in six countries, co-edits the *South Sydney Herald* and participates in various human rights activities, including those for homosexual people, like herself.

> I have discovered that the religious quest is not about discovering 'the truth' or 'the meaning of life', but about living as intensely as possible in the here and now ... A passing Brahmin priest once asked the Buddha whether he was a god, a spirit, or an angel. None of these, the Buddha replied: 'I am awake!' ... In the past, my own practice of religion has diminished me, whereas true faith, I now believe, should make you more human than before.
>
> Karen Armstrong

Reflections

This reflection by Karen Armstrong reminds me of an iconic moment in my life with a young woman from the Philippines called Jessica Sales. She had given a workshop on her work with the families of political prisoners of the then President Marcos. I asked her how the workshop went and she said, 'It went well, Dorothy, but I think those words could cost me my life.' Then she paused and said firmly, 'But I have to live.' A day later she was arrested, tortured and later killed by the Philippines military. I knew that she had lived more in her twenty-two years than I would ever live.

Jessica was an example of what lies at the very heart of my faith – that life is full of death and resurrection patterns and that the ultimate calling is to live with courage and hope, even as you 'die'. I have been privileged to meet several people who have died or been imprisoned as they stood for justice for their people and the other quality they have all had was one of profound humanness. I will never tread their brave road, but they are my inspiration.

⬤ Excerpt from Karen Armstrong, *The Spiral Staircase*, Harper Perennial, London. Reprinted by permission of HarperCollins Publishers Ltd © Karen Armstrong 2005.
Karen Armstrong (1945–) is an ex-nun, a feminist and a prolific scholar of religions. Her most famous book is *A History of God*.
Dorothy also chose *I Will not Die an Unlived Life* (see page 152)

MALA MEHTA, OAM

Indian-born Mala worked with a team of dedicated teachers and supportive parents to pioneer a formal teaching program of the Hindi language, founding the Indo-Aust Bal Bharathi Vidyalaya Hindi School in Sydney. The school operates as an incorporated non-profit organisation, supported by the New South Wales Department of Training and Education.

> Where the mind is without fear and the head is held high;
> Where knowledge is free;
> Where the world has not been broken up into fragments
> by narrow domestic walls;
> Where words come out from the depth of truth;
> Where tireless striving stretches its arms towards
> perfection;
> Where the clear stream of reason has not lost its way
> into the dreary desert sand of dead habit;
> Where the mind is led forward by thee into ever-widening
> thought and action-
> Into that heaven of freedom, my Father, let my country
> awake.
>
> Rabindranath Tagore

Reflections

The poem by Tagore I have quoted has been a favourite since school and I have actually danced to it along with our school choir. In an unconscious way it probably has been my guiding force.

I also feel very strongly about providing our children with a safe and loving environment in which to grow as well as giving them ample opportunities through which they can contribute to the nation, integrating and enriching this great multicultural Australia that we call home. It is my conviction that deep concepts can only be understood by knowing the language. When you live in a country with a dominant language, any minority language must naturally come under threat. It requires effort on the part of parents to keep the second or third or fourth language alive.

I share the belief with one of my teachers Shobha Sharma, that 'languages taught in schools should reflect the community; language is a doorway to understanding a people and their culture'. 'Intolerance', she writes, 'nearly always comes from lack of education and understanding – surely reason enough to learn any language.'

●Rabindranath Tagore, 'Where the Mind is Without Fear', in *Gitanjali*, a collection of 103 inspirational poems.
Rabindranath Tagore (1861–1941) was an Indian poet, playwright and essayist. In 1913, he won the Nobel Prize in Literature.

○○○

JIM MEIN

Jim was a partner in a national chartered accountancy firm. In 2004, he was elected first full-time moderator at the Uniting Church New South Wales Synod. During his three-year term as moderator, Jim has been an active advocate of inter-faith dialogue, particularly in engagements with the Muslim community.

Not that I have already obtained this or have already reached the goal; but I press on to make it my own, because Christ Jesus has made me his own. Beloved, I do not consider that I have made it my own; but this one thing I do: forgetting what lies behind and straining forward to what lies ahead, I press on toward the goal for the prize of the heavenly call of God in Christ Jesus.

Let those of us then who are mature be of the same mind; and if you think differently about anything, this too God will reveal to you. Only let us hold fast to what we have attained.

Philippians 3:12–16 New Revised Standard Version Bible

Reflections

I love using sporting anecdotes and images to inspire young Christian leaders. My favourite inspiration comes from Philippians and it combines my two special interests (besides being a 'sportaholic') – 'change' and 'strategy'. Here, Paul moves from talking about breaking with the past (change) to pressing towards the goal (strategy) 'the prize of the heavenly call of God in Christ Jesus'.

In rugby, there is a tactical kick called the 'up and under'. The attacking team kick a very high ball towards their try-scoring end, so the team can move fast downfield as the ball is airborne, hoping one of them can catch it and score a try. The 'up and under' involves change (the tactical variation) and strategy (how to achieve the goal of a try).

As Christians, we must show God's unconditional love to the homeless, under-privileged, suffering and disadvantaged, the 'down-and-outers'. If we look 'up' to Jesus for inspiration, and at the same time we include the 'down-and-outers' in our care before the ball comes down for us to catch, we will be working towards our goal – of eternal life in Jesus Christ. The church is for 'up-and-unders' and 'down-and-outers', for there is room for everyone.

Another of my sporting anecdotes involves the goal of successfully clearing a high-jump bar by aiming higher than the bar. The strategy involves focusing on your goal and includes the run-up approach to the bar, the power of your take-off and the movement of your whole body up and over the bar. Much planning, self-talk, self-analysis and, for me, prayer is required to remain purposeful and in control of the butterflies flying about inside me.

The church will not grow unless we aim higher. This involves change and strategy to achieve what God wants the church to be: past-preserving gatekeepers must change to being 'up-and-unders' who welcome all people, even 'down-and-outers'.

OOO

DOCTOR
HARRY MELKONIAN

Educator and solicitor Harry Melkonian is national moderator of the Congregational Federation of Australian and New Zealand and a lay minister in the Congregational Church. He has a masters degree in astronomy and a doctorate in law. He teaches American history at Sydney University's Centre for Continuing Education.

> **God answers every prayer,**
> **but sometimes the answer is no.**
>
> **Anonymous**

Reflections

God's wisdom is beyond our understanding. Sometimes, when our prayers are not granted, we think that God is not listening; but he is listening and always answers. However, sometimes his answer is beyond our understanding.

○○○

RICHARD MENTEITH, AM

Richard is the national president of Churches of Christ in Australia and chief financial officer for the Wesley Mission. His wrote his masters' thesis on organisational structure, and uses these skills to assist many organisations, including the Sydney College of Divinity and the Newcastle City Mission.

The earth is the Lord's,
and the fullness thereof ...
It speaks of His greatness –
it sings of His love.
And each day at dawning,
I lift my heart high
And raise up my eyes
to the infinite sky.
I watch the night vanish
as a new day is born,
And I hear the birds sing
on the wings of the morn.
I see the dew glisten
in crystal-like splendor
While God, with a touch
that is gentle and tender,
Wraps up the night
and softly tucks it away
And hangs out the sun
to herald a new day ...
And so I give thanks
and my heart kneels to pray,
'God, keep me and guide me
and go with me today.'

Helen Steiner Rice

Reflections

The passage reminds me of several characteristics of a loving father. It reminds me that God is the creator and all things are within his control. It reminds me of the gentle loving nature of God and that as I commit each moment of each day to him, he will faithfully walk with me and sustain me throughout the new day regardless of the challenges I face.

○○○

HARRY M MILLER

A well-known promoter, publicist and entrepreneur, Harry M Miller represents a number of prominent Australian personalities. He has produced many theatrical productions in Australia, including *Jesus Christ Superstar*, *The Rocky Horror Show* and *Hair*. He is a Raja yoga practitioner.

Anybody who wants to be instrumental in serving the world needs to know how to work with integrity. Integrity elevates character and brings internal power. It reveals a pure attitude. Those with integrity maintain great humility, even while holding positions of high status and commanding a lot of respect. They do not alter their character or virtues according to whom they are with. They have pride in themselves.

Integrity over a long period of time makes the soul powerful. The intellect is clear and does not mix truth with falsehood. A person with integrity is able to reveal truth through words spoken with wisdom. They never feel the need to prove truth. Because a clear conscience is the reward of such honesty, a person with integrity considers the consequences of every action and is never drawn mindlessly into anything. To behave in a lesser way is to deceive people.

Dadi Janki

Reflections

I think Dadi Janki is one of our wisest and most influential leaders. She sets an example for all of us.

●Dadi Janki, 'Integrity', from 'Love and Relationships III' in *Companion of God: the wisdom and words of Dadi Janki*, Brahma Kumaris Centre, Australia. (Retrieved from athilat.com/bkwsu/Integrity.htm)

Dadi Janki (1916–) is internationally acknowledged as a great teacher and mentor. She is one of ten Keepers of Wisdom, an eminent group of world spiritual leaders who advised the Earth Summit in 1992 in Brazil.

OOO

MIKE MUNRO

After a challenging childhood involving poverty, alcoholism and emotional deprivation, Mike embarked on a journalism career when he was seventeen years old. He has reported from locations around the world and has hosted a number of television programs, including *60 Minutes*, *A Current Affair* and *This Is Your Life*.

Hail Mary, full of grace, the Lord is with thee.
Blessed art thou among women, and blessed is the
fruit of thy womb, Jesus.

Holy Mary, Mother of God, pray for us sinners,
now and at the hour of our death.

Amen.

Hail Mary, traditional version

Reflections

Growing up, I continually prayed to Mary to make my mother sober after twenty-eight years of alcoholism. She eventually died an alcoholic, but Mary did provide me with the perfect childhood sweetheart – who later became my wife – two beautiful children and a wonderful career.

● The Hail Mary is a popular prayer among Roman Catholics; it is the essential element of the rosary, a prayer method practised primarily by Catholics calling for the intercession of Mary, the mother of Jesus. The first sentence is the greeting of the Archangel Gabriel to Mary (Luke 1:28). The second is the greeting to Mary by her cousin, Elizabeth, in Luke 1:42. It is also a reinforcement of basic Christian belief in the real divinity and real humanity of Jesus. The closing two lines came into general use in the sixteenth century.

ELISABETH MURDOCH, AC, DBE

Elisabeth is the widow of Australian newspaper publisher Sir Keith Murdoch and mother of international media magnate Rupert Murdoch. She is celebrated for her philanthropy. She is patron of the Murdoch Children's Research Institute, founding member of the Deafness Foundation of Victoria and the Victorian Tapestry Workshop.

To every thing there is a season, and a time to every purpose under the heaven:

A time to be born, and a time to die; a time to plant, and a time to pluck up that which is planted;

A time to kill, and a time to heal; a time to break down, and a time to build up;

A time to weep, and a time to laugh; a time to mourn, and a time to dance;

A time to cast away stones, and a time to gather stones together; a time to embrace, and a time to refrain from embracing;

A time to get, and a time to lose; a time to keep, and a time to cast away;

A time to rend, and a time to sew; a time to keep silence, and a time to speak;

A time to love, and a time to hate; a time of war, and a time of peace.

Ecclesiastes 3:1–8 King James Bible

Reflections

This bible passage expresses my feelings about life.

OOO

LES MURRAY, AO

One of Australia's leading poets, Les Murray has won numerous literary awards, including the Grace Leven Prize, the Petrarch Prize and the prestigious TS Eliot Award. In 1999, he was awarded the Queen's Gold Medal for Poetry. His work has been published in ten languages.

> **The true god gives his flesh and blood.**
> **Idols demand yours off you.**
>
> **Les Murray**

Reflections

I was proud to capture, in verse, this distinction between the divine mercy and the ghastly en-masse human sacrifices people often offer up to their political or other inspirations.

⬤Excerpt from Les Murray, 'Church', in *The Biplane Houses*, Black Inc., Melbourne, 2006.

RON NATOLI

A builder for more than forty years, Ron is committed to assisting disadvantaged people in the Philippines, through the development organisation Bethlehem Communities Australia. He is interested in the effect of spiritual influences on daily life, and ways in which we can choose to use this to benefit ourselves and others.

Dear Lord,

I thank you for the wonderful people you surround me with; for those 'chance' or 'coincidental' introductions to people that seem to be so vital to my personal development and the progress of your work – you are the spirit that moves and guides – we are your hands.
I pray for all these people, dear Lord, knowing that when you are involved, nothing happens by chance.
Please continue to inspire and guide me to do your will.

Amen.

Ron Natoli

Reflections

I realise how significant those around us are in helping us achieve our goals, and I have discovered that when we pray for help it is always given. God brings the right person into our lives at the appropriate time. In gratitude for this, we offer our 'human hands' to him: to be guided by the Spirit and to do his will.

When we offer ourselves in this way, God will use us and our talents to accomplish his goals. Without doubt, he is all-powerful. He uses our 'human hands' to bring his projects and goals to life.

JOHN NEWCOMBE, AO, OBE

Dominating the world tennis circuit during the 1960s and 1970s, John Newcome reached number one in the world tennis rankings, winning multiple Wimbledon, US and Australian Open tournaments. He is one of only two players to win both the US Open and Wimbledon men's singles titles as an amateur and as a professional.

If you can keep your head when all about you
Are losing theirs and blaming it on you,
If you can trust yourself when all men doubt you,
But make allowance for their doubting too;
If you can wait and not be tired by waiting,
Or being lied about, don't deal in lies,
Or being hated, don't give way to hating,
And yet don't look too good, nor talk too wise:

If you can dream – and not make dreams your master;
If you can think – and not make thoughts your aim;
If you can meet with Triumph and Disaster
And treat those two impostors just the same;
If you can bear to hear the truth you've spoken
Twisted by knaves to make a trap for fools,
Or watch the things you gave your life to, broken,
And stoop and build 'em up with worn-out tools:

If you can make one heap of all your winnings
And risk it on one turn of pitch-and-toss,
And lose, and start again at your beginnings
And never breathe a word about your loss;
If you can force your heart and nerve and sinew
To serve your turn long after they are gone,
And so hold on when there is nothing in you
Except the Will which says to them: 'Hold on!'

continued overleaf

If you can talk with crowds and keep your virtue,
Or walk with Kings – nor lose the common touch,
If neither foes nor loving friends can hurt you,
If all men count with you, but none too much;
If you can fill the unforgiving minute
With sixty seconds' worth of distance run,
Yours is the Earth and everything that's in it,
And – which is more – you'll be a Man, my son!

Rudyard Kipling

Reflections

This is my favourite poem. And these two lines from it are inscribed above the door at the entrance to Centre Court at Wimbledon:

'If you can meet with Triumph and Disaster
And treat those two impostors just the same'

Rudyard Kippling, 'If–', from the chapter, 'Brother Square-Toes', in *Rewards and Fairies*. First published 1910.

Rudyard Kipling (1865–1936) was a British author and poet. He was best known for his children's books *The Jungle Book* and *Just So Stories*.

OOO

JACQUELINE NINIO

Jacqueline practised law before beginning her five-year rabbinical training. She is the third Australian-born woman to be ordained as a rabbi and has been working at Temple Emanuel in Sydney for the past eight years.

And then all that has divided us will merge
And then compassion will be wedded to power
And then softness will come to a world that is harsh
and unkind
And then both men and women will be gentle
And then both women and men will be strong
And then no person will be subject to another's will
And then all will be rich and free and varied
And then the greed of some will give way to the needs
of many
And then all will share equally in the earth's abundance
And then all will care for the sick and the weak and the old
And then all will nourish the young
And then all will cherish life's creatures
And then all will live in harmony with each other and
the earth
And then everywhere will be called Eden once again.

Judy Chicago

Reflections

I love this prayer for its universal message and inclusiveness. It expresses my hope for the world. The dream of this prayer will only happen, I believe, if we work together to make the world a reflection of the Eden for which we long. It will not happen if we sit and wait. We need to be proactive, and for me this prayer also acts as a call to action.

⬤ The poem *Merger* by Judy Chicago, Reconstructionist Jewish Prayer book, Kol Haneshamah: Shabbat Vehagim 2nd edn, Reconstructionist Press, Pennsylvania, 1995. © 2007 Judy Chicago/Artsists Rights Society (ARS), New York.
  Judy Chicago (1979–) is an American artist, author, feminist, educator and intellectual.

CLIVE NORTON

Anglican priest Clive Norton has shared with his wife, Ruth, over forty-eight years of fulfilling ministry to people and parishes, in education and community organisations. He feels indebted to the inclusive tradition of the Anglican Church and the corrective inspiration and wisdom of the Ecumenical Movement.

Praise the restless, roving Spirit,
breeze of Christ and breath of God,
kindling faith and power to share it,
quick to comfort, nudge and prod!

Culture's heroes tempt and lure us,
smashing wrong with righteous force,
but the wounds of Christ can cure us,
marking out a wiser course.

Spirit, give us Christ's persistence;
raise us when our spirit cowers,
freed for peaceful, firm resistance
to our world's corrupted powers.

Keep us hopeful and forgiving,
loving when we disagree,
by our liturgy and living
hinting how the world will be.

Brian Wren

Reflections

It confronts us as we sit back in apathy or rush in like fools (in our pride). Many people today are anxious and seek certainties. We are barraged by religious, political and economic one-dimensional men (and some women!) trying to sell their brand of fundamentalism/literalism/prophecies: to give 'simple' answers and tell us what to do. Jesus Christ refused that way. The Spirit that Christ embodied can teach us how to act and lead us to truth.

⬤ Brian Wren, 'Praise the Restless, Roving Spirit' © Hope Publishing Company. Used with permission of Clive and Ruth Norton. Brian Wren (1936–) hymn-writer and theologian, wrote this prayer-hymn to celebrate Clive Norton's continuing ministry when he retired from the Anglican parish of Hunters Hill in Sydney.

SIR
GUSTAV NOSSAL, AC, CBE

Gustav is a distinguished research biologist who has conducted groundbreaking work in immunology. He holds numerous international scientific awards and doctorates and was Australian of the Year in 2000. Gustav currently works in international health with the Bill and Melinda Gates Foundation and the World Health Organization.

> Blessed are they which do hunger and thirst after righteousness: for they shall be filled.
>
> Blessed are the peacemakers: for they shall be called the children of God.
>
> Blessed are they which are persecuted for righteousness' sake: for theirs is the kingdom of heaven.
>
> Matthew 5: 6, 9–10 King James Bible

Reflections

In these troubled times, the thirst for global social justice is intense. We have each of us, in our own way, to seek to make a better world, even if our actions are unpopular. As the late Pope John Paul said, 'Peace is an instrument of justice.'

OOO

PROFESSOR
GERALD O'COLLINS, SJ, AC

Born in Melbourne, Gerald was ordained as a priest in 1963, received his doctorate in 1968, and taught theology at the Gregorian University in Rome for thirty-two years. The author of forty-eight books, he is a research professor in theology at St Mary's University College, Twickenham in the United Kingdom.

Thanks be to thee, my Lord Jesus Christ, for all the benefits which thou hast given me – for all the pains and insults thou hast borne for me.

O most merciful Redeemer, Friend and Brother, may I know thee more clearly, love thee more dearly, and follow thee more nearly.

St Richard of Chichester

Reflections

This prayer expresses very tenderly and personally deep gratitude towards Christ for his love in accepting suffering and death for us. There is a wonderful sequence in 'Redeemer, Friend and Brother'. Jesus is not only our redeemer but also our friend and even our brother.

This prayer is found in front of the tomb of St Richard (1197–1253), which is situated behind the high altar in the Cathedral of Chichester, England.
Gerald O'Collins also chose the Lord's Prayer (see page 46).

OOO

JOHN OLSEN, OBE, AO

John is one of Australia's most significant and accomplished artists and is recognised both nationally and internationally. His mural *Salute to Five Bells* hangs in the Sydney Opera House. John has won many awards, including the 2005 Archibald Prize for his self-portrait. He writes that he has had 'a life spent in appreciation of nature's splendour'.

Glory be to God for dappled things –
For skies of couple-colour as a brinded cow;
For rose-moles all in stipple upon trout that swim;
Fresh-firecoal chestnut-falls; finches' wings;
Landscape plotted and pieced – fold, fallow, and plough;
And áll trades, their gear and tackle and trim.

All things counter, original, spáre, strange;
Whatever is fickle, frecklèd (who knows how?)
With swíft, slów; sweet, sóur; adázzle, dím;
He fathers-forth whose beauty is pást change:
Práise hím.

Gerard Manley Hopkins

Reflections

Whenever I speak publicly, I begin with this poem. I am moved by the vision and tone of this poem which so beautifully expresses the diversity and grace of nature. As French author and aviator Antoine de Saint-Exupéry (1900–44) wrote: 'The meaning of things lies not in the things themselves, but in our attitude towards them.'

● Gerard Manley Hopkins, 'Pied Beauty'. First published in 1877.
Gerard Manley Hopkins (1844–89) was a poet and priest.

○○○

SUSIE O'NEILL

Former Olympic swimmer Susie O'Neill holds a staggering record thirty-five Australian titles and eight Olympic medals. Her 1996 gold medal win at the Atlanta Olympics was the first ever for an Australian woman in Olympic competition in the 200-metre butterfly, and thereby attributing her the famous nickname of 'Madame Butterfly' for her extraordinary number of wins in both the 100- and 200-metre events. Retired from swimming, Susie is an now ambassador for The Fred Hollows Foundation.

There are four corners on your bed,
There are four angels overhead.
Matthew, Mark, Luke and John,
God bless this bed [name*] lies on.

* name of whoever you say it to

Reflections

My nanna used to say this to me when I was going to bed at her place. It made me feel relaxed and very special. I was very close to her.

● Susie also chose 'Always treat others as you would like to be treated.' (see page 172).

◯◯◯

MEHMET OZALP

Mehmet, developer of many courses on Islam and personal leadership, has a passion for inter-faith issues. A founding director of Affinity Intercultural Foundation, he was a member of the Community Harmony Reference Group with the Community Relations Commission in Sydney, established by the premier of New South Wales in 2003.

My Lord, to you I complain of my weakness and lack of ability, my being scorned by others.
Most Merciful of the Merciful, you are the Lord of the oppressed and my Lord as well.
Who have you given me to?
To strangers who insult me or to an enemy that dominates me?
If you are angry with me, I don't mind, but your pardon is the most important thing I desire.
I seek the help of the light of your visage that dispels darkness and sustains both this world and the next.
In that I take refuge.
I pray that your wrath does not befall me nor your displeasure overtake me.
To you alone belongs the right to blame and to chastise until your pleasure is met.
There is no power or strength save in you.

Prophet Muhammad

Reflections

This prayer is made by the Prophet Muhammad as a result of suffering he endured in a town called Ta'if. At a time when he and his followers were tortured and oppressed, he travelled to Ta'if looking for support. Not only did the leaders of the town humiliate the Prophet, they also arranged for children to pelt rocks at him. He was severely bruised and wounded so that blood ran down into his shoes.

Narratives report that the Angel Gabriel offered to turn the mountain onto the town if the Prophet wished. But the Prophet Muhammad did not agree and made this prayer instead.

There is immense wisdom in this prayer, revealing how to approach God in times of hardship and suffering at the hands of others. The Prophet seeks no vengeance but focuses on his own state and his relationship with God. He wonders if he has deserved this treatment. He seeks the pleasure of God. He asks for God to strengthen him, not to destroy others.

● Excerpt from Yahiya Emerick, *Critical Lives: Muhammad*, Alpha Books, 2002. © Yahiya Emerick. Reprinted with permisssion of Alpha Books, an imprint of Penguin Books (USA). US Author Yahiya Emerick is a convert to Islam.

○○○

CAROL PALMER

Carol was drawn to the Church from childhood and from the late 1990s she discovered Christ. In 2006 she was ordained as a priest in Grafton Cathedral and is currently assistant priest in the Anglican Parish of Murwillumbah. Carol is a former teacher, chorister and occasional organist.

Priestly life is nothing more nor less than the fulfilling of our deepest longings, rooted in our capacity for being human. The great purpose of human existence is to enjoy communion with God and with God's creation ... namely with one another ...

This priestly existence, however, is not automatic. Like every human excellence, we have to practise it, reflect on it, and grow into it. This process is what we call 'spirituality'. It is the process of becoming more aware of who and where we really are and of learning to look for the HIDDEN HOLY in and under the busyness of everyday existence. What we can do however, is make ourselves open and available for the conversation with the TRANSCENDENT and with one another.

To enter upon this journey requires an increasingly strong sense of self ... a self that springs from God's creative grace and is sustained by God's continuing goodness. Only such a self can participate in the loving exchange of gifts, the profound conversation that lies at the heart of what it means to be human.

L William Countryman

Reflections

My journey in Christ began in the early 1980s after a dramatic conversion, following three decades of questioning, doubt and nominal Anglicanism. The past two years have been energising, as God's plan has gradually and prayerfully unfolded, and I have felt showered with blessings. A 'wounded healer' – the term coined by Henri Nouwen (1932-1996), renowned priest and author – I feel I have come home to full-time ministry as a graced opportunity and a humble challenge. Countryman's words, both poignant and profound, have helped me to articulate and make sense of the process of journeying with Christ.

● Excerpt from L William Countryman, *Living on the Border of the Holy: renewing the priesthood of all*, Morehouse Publishing, Philadelphia, 1999.

LW Countryman is an author and an Episcopal priest in America. He is professor of biblical studies, Church Divinity School of the Pacific, Berkeley, California.

GEORGE PELL

George was ordained a priest in 1966 and holds a licentiate in theology, a doctorate of philosophy in church history, and a masters degree in education. He has been the Roman Catholic archbishop of Sydney since 2001 and a cardinal of the Roman Catholic Church since 2003.

Remember O most loving Virgin Mary,
that never was it known in any age,
that anyone who fled to your protection,
implored your help,
or sought your intercession,
was abandoned.
Inspired with confidence,
therefore, I fly to you
O Virgin of virgins, my Mother,
to you do I come,
before you I stand,
sinful and sorrowful; do not,
O Mother of the Word incarnate,
despise my prayers,
but graciously hear and grant them.
Amen.

Attributed to St Bernard of Clairvaux

Reflections

Even though the style of this passage is a bit old-fashioned, I have been saying it since I was taught it by the Christian Brothers as a teenager. I always use it as a prayer going into and coming out of mass.

● St Bernard, 'The Memorare'.
    This is a very popular Marian prayer. St Bernard of Clairvaux (1090–1153) was a French Abbot and doctor of the church.

○○○

PETA JONES PELLACH

Peta is director of Adult Education at The Shalom Institute at the University of New South Wales. She is a consultant to the Executive Council of Australian Jewry and a delegate on a number of inter-faith dialogues. She is committed to inter-faith cooperation and understanding.

We offer thanks, O Lord Our G-d, for the miracles that You have performed for us – in the past, in the present, in every generation.

We thank You for allowing small minorities to flourish – even in the face of large, powerful forces.

We thank You for allowing us to celebrate our faiths, in our own ways.

On this first night of Chanukah, our candle burns symbolically for the miracle of survival and for the joy of reaching this season.

Blessed are You, O Lord our G-d, Who has enabled us to reach this season of joy, Who has extended us favours and granted us life.

Peta Jones Pellach

Reflections

On Chanukah 2004, I was privileged to light candles in Jogjakarta, Indonesia, and was able to recite my own words of blessing in the presence of my fellow delegates to the Regional Dialogue for Interfaith Cooperation, in the palace of the Sultan.

My prayer was heartfelt and it was my intention to express my gratitude to G-d for guiding my life to that auspicious moment, when I represented both my country, Australia, and my Jewish faith.

GREGORY PHILLIPS

Indigenous Australian Gregory Phillips is a member of the Waanyi nation from Lawn Hills, Mount Isa and Cloncurry in northwest Queensland. A community healing worker, medical anthropologist, author and researcher, he has worked with Indigenous people around the world helping them reconnect with their spiritual and cultural roots and heal from the traumas of colonisation, alcohol and drugs.

> Aboriginal people believe that the spirit child comes from the earth ... We come from this earth, we are born of the earth. We believe that the whole of life is a spiritual experience and that we as Aboriginal people are actually more spirit than matter.
>
> Aunty Lilla Watson

Reflections

Praying in the religious sense is not a traditional Aboriginal cultural phenomenon, but our people practised a kind of meditation where we 'talked', or communicated, to the ancestral spirits and creator beings – and to nature itself. If we quiet ourselves enough, the land talks to us, even today. This is a central tenet of the spirituality, law and religion of many Aboriginal people: if you humble yourself to the land and the Old Ones, if you quiet yourself enough in the right way, then the land will tell you what you need to know; you will sense it as much as hear it or see it.

Aunty Lilla, a strong Indigenous elder, is telling us where we come from, and that to live life well as an Aboriginal person you have to listen to the spiritual, and see your existence as important to the generations to come, rather than merely as a human being now.

This passage is among my mainstays. It helps keep me grounded, and I return to it for inspiration and direction in life.

⬤ Aunty Lilla Watson, Indigenous elder from Queensland, interviewed by Gregory Phillips, in *Addictions and Healing in Aboriginal Country*, Aboriginal Studies Press, Canberra, 2003.

○○○

GREIG PICKHAVER

Popular ABC Radio and Television personality Greig Pickhaver is better known as 'HG', who along with 'Roy Slaven' (John Doyle), form the successful Australian comedy duo Roy and HG. Together they have presented various programs, such as *This Sporting Life* and *Club Buggery*. Greig supports many charities, including The Asylum Seekers Centre in Sydney.

If my words did glow with the gold of sunshine,
And my tunes were played on the harp unstrung,
Would you hear my voice come through the music
Would you hold it near as it were your own?

It's a hand-me-down, the thoughts are broken,
Perhaps they're better left unsung.
I don't know, don't really care,
Let there be songs to fill the air.

Ripple in still water,
When there is no pebble tossed,
Nor wind to blow.

Reach out your hand if your cup be empty,
If your cup is full may it be again,
Let it be known there is a fountain,
That was not made by the hands of men.

There is a road, no simple highway,
Between the dawn and the dark of night,
And if you go no one may follow,
That path is for your steps alone.

Ripple in still water,
When there is no pebble tossed,
Nor wind to blow.

continued overleaf

You who choose to lead must follow,
But if you fall you fall alone.
If you should stand then who's to guide you?
If I knew the way I would take you home.

Robert Hunter

● 'Ripple', lyrics by Robert Hunter, music by Jerry Garcia, as performed by the Grateful Dead. Reproduced by arrangement with Ice Nine Publishing Company Inc., San Rafael, California (iceninepublishing.com).
Robert Hunter is a singer, songwriter, poet, author, husband, and father. He was the chief lyricist of the Grateful Dead throughout their career. He wrote 'Ripple' in the folksong tradition during the late 1960s.

○○○

SUE PIETERS-HAWKE

Daughter of former Labour Prime Minister Bob Hawke, Sue works as a speaker, coach, consultant and advocate. She co-wrote the bestselling *Hazel's Journey: a personal experience of Alzheimer's* about her mother, Hazel Hawke. She has studied law, history, complementary health and healing, yoga, qigong and Tibetan Buddhism and escapes into her garden or a book at any excuse.

Grant me the serenity to accept the things
I cannot change,
Courage to change the things I can and
Wisdom to know the difference.

Attributed to Reinhold Niebuhr

Reflections

I have used these words as a heartfelt prayer during tough times, but for me, they also represent an approach to living which resonates deeply.

● Excerpt from Reinhold Niebuhr, 'The Serenity Prayer'.
Reinhold Niebuhr (1892–1971) never claimed 'The Serenity Prayer' as his own. It could well date to eighteenth century or earlier.

BEVERLEY POLZIN

Beverley is an Australian who joined the Religious Society of Friends, or Quakers, while living in Cornwall, England in 1981. For six years she was the Yearly Meeting secretary, the sole employee of Quakers in Australia. Prior to this, she worked in the welfare and community sector.

> They that love beyond the world, cannot be separated by it. Death cannot kill, what never dies.
>
> Nor can Spirits ever be divided that love and live in the same Divine Principle; the root and record of their friendship.
>
> If absence be not death, neither is theirs.
>
> Death is but crossing the world, as friends do the seas; They live in one another still.
>
> For they must needs be present, that love and live in that which is Omnipresent.
>
> In this divine glass they see face to face; and their converse is free, as well as pure.
>
> This is the comfort of friends, that though they may be said to die, yet their friendship and society are, in the best sense, ever present, because immortal.
>
> William Penn

Reflections

This passage is one that Friends often quote at Quaker funerals. It offers a sense of unity between life and death and a bridge over the mystery of death for those whose connection has been grounded in love.

I believe these words have the power to comfort souls beyond the borders of the Religious Society of Friends and are the fruits of the life of a true mystic.

● Excerpt from 'Part II: reflections and maxims', in *Fruits of Solitude*, Vol. I, Part 3, The Harvard Classics, PF Collier & Son, New York, 1909–14.
William Penn (1644–1718) was an English mystic and staunch peace advocate.

○○○

DOCTOR
MURIEL PORTER, OAM

Muriel is an Anglican laywoman, a leading advocate for the ordination of women and a church historian and journalist. A member of the Anglican Church's national governing body, the General Synod, since 1987, and its Standing Committee since 1989, Muriel is also a member of the General Synod Doctrine Commission.

> It suddenly strikes me
> with overwhelming force:
>
> It was women
> who were the first to spread the message
> of Easter –
> The unheard of!
>
> It was women
> who rushed to the disciples,
> who, breathless and bewildered,
> passed on the greatest message of all:
>
> He is alive!
>
> Think if women had kept silence
> in the churches!
>
> Märta Wilhelmsson

Reflections

I came across this poem about twenty years ago at the height of the debate over women priests in the Anglican Church. I have kept it pinned up over my desk ever since. It continually inspires me to keep up the struggle for women, reminding me that women were the first 'apostles to the apostles!' They were, and are, commissioned by our Lord himself.

●Märta Wilhelmsson, 'Messengers', in 'No Longer Strangers: a resource of women and worship', eds. Iben Gjerding and Katherine Kinnamon, World Council of Churches, 1983. Used with permission.

CHESTER PORTER, QC

In 1948, at the age of twenty-one, Chester was one of the youngest lawyers to be admitted to the bar. He is regarded as a legal thinker with the moral courage to question criminal law. In 1986, Chester was Rostrum Speaker of the Year.

> The Lord of Hosts is with us; the God of Jacob
> is our refuge.
>
> Psalm 46:7 King James Bible

Reflections

It is so easy to lose confidence in oneself and in the world. It is easy to be fearful in times of trouble. This verse supplies an answer.

○○○

BOB RANDALL

An elder of the Yankunytjatjara people, Bob Randall – also known as Uncle Bob – is a listed traditional owner of Uluru. At a young age, he was taken away from his mother, becoming one of the 'Stolen Generation'. Bob is a former director of the Northern Australia Legal Aid Service and established Aboriginal and Torres Strait Islander centres at several Australian universities. In 1999, he was named Indigenous Person of the Year. In 2006, Bob presented and co-produced the film *Kanyini* with Melanie Hogan (see Melanie's entry on page 87).

> The earth is our mother. We are born from her. She looks after us with meat, bush tucker as well as water. To us the purpose of life is to be part of all that there is. You had this discipline in place – of not to take more than you need. Being alive connects you to every other living thing that's around you, your spirit, your psyche, your physical, your mental, you're all connected with other living forms. My people have always been part of the earth. Every single inch of this land and its waterways is sacred land.

continued overleaf

Then everything changed, we changed. We started to shrink. The government took away *Kanyini* which is the connectedness from me to four concepts:

Tjukurpa, which is my belief system,
my *kurunpa* which is my spirituality,
my land which is my *ngura* and
my family which is my *walytja*.

I've got to connect with each of these four lines to be whole. You take away my *Kanyini*, my connectedness, my life, my essence of all I'm here for, my purpose, you take that away, and I'm nothing. I become nothing and that's what the government did, it took away that *Kanyini*. We can't go back to the old ways, because the natural environment has been destroyed. Nothing is there in its natural state was when I was a child.

As the concepts were damaged and the responsibilities taken away, we need to now strengthen those, from me, with my responsibility, my *Kanyini*, strengthen it, connecting with my family and connecting with my land – and you can come with me, we can do it together. Strengthening with my belief system and strengthening with my spirituality. Because really, it's our right, yours and mine, as being born human, to have the sense of belonging, which carries the responsibility which we call *Kanyini*.

Bob Randall

Reflections

When all people desire to get to know each other as family members, peace can exist among us all, regardless of our differences and our similarities. *Kanyini* can allow this to happen and we'll meet each other there. Once we change the way we think, our spirit then helps us to make the necessary changes in the way we live. But to get that help we have to accept *Kanyini* – love and responsibility for all things.

● Excerpt from Bob Randall's narration in *Kanyini*. *Kanyini* is a Pitjantjatjara word – it means interconnectedness; to care for, and to nurture and support. The film depicts Bob's personal journey as an Indigenous Australian and the wisdom gained from Indigenous elders in the bush. The film was directed by Melanie Hogan, Reverb Films (kanyini.com).

MAHBOBA RAWI

An Afghan refugee, Mahboba lost her son to drowning two years after coming to Australia. She is the driving force behind 'Mahboba's Promise Inc', an aid organisation that delivers food, shelter, medical attention, education and hope to hundreds of children and women whose lives have been destroyed by war in Afghanistan.

> O Lord, give me a heart
> I can pour out in thanksgiving.
> Give me life
> So I can spend it
> Working for the salvation of the world
>
> Sheikh Ansari

Reflections

I have selected this particular verse as I feel it reflects my attitude to living my life. It also affirms my belief in my work with orphans and widows, which I consider is my destiny and vocation. Such prayers serve as a source of inspiration and strength in my moments of doubt and anxiety. My life is dedicated to serving those in need.

● Sheikh Ansari, 'Give Me', in Andrew Harvey and Eryk Hanut, *Perfume of the Desert: inspirations from Sufi wisdom*, Quest Books, Illinois, 1999. Reproduced by permission of Quest Books, the imprint of The Theosopical Publishing House (questbooks.net).
Sheikh Ansari (1006–88) was a known scholar of his era.

ADEN RIDGEWAY

Aden is a proud member of the Gumbayyngirr people from the north coast of New South Wales. When he was elected as Democrat senator for New South Wales in 1998, he was Australia's only Indigenous federal politician. From April 2001 until October 2002 he served as deputy leader of the Democrat Party.

I will not die an unlived life.
I will not live in fear
of falling or catching fire.
I choose to inhabit my days,
to allow my living to open me,
to make me less afraid,
more accessible,
to loosen my heart
until it becomes a wing,
a torch, a promise.
I choose to risk my significance;
to live so that which came to me as seed
goes to the next as blossom
and that which came to me as blossom,
goes on as fruit.

Dawna Markova

Reflections

I believe that we are a part of a much bigger connectedness. Most of the time it is incomprehensible but there are moments in our life when we experience perfect synchronicity and clarity. You feel it on those days when everything seems to line up, and no matter the presence of ongoing mundane problems, everything feels alive ... your whole body comes to life and you radiate this unseen energy. It is a moment when your whole outlook on life changes and even the thought of getting a parking ticket during the day seems to fade into insignificance and you give thanks to the smaller things that make your life so brilliant: a smile from a passing stranger, a cold drink on a hot summer's day, the sound of the wind blowing through the leaves or even dancing with your little five-year-old.

Isn't this what life is about?

Dawna Markova's inspirational piece speaks to me about how life should be lived and how we should take the risk of surrendering and living a life full of passion to ourselves and to others. I think it is far too easy for many to say that this is not possible but, I believe, the reality is that many are too afraid to try or are preoccupied with too many other things in their lives.

Go on … 'Life, Be in It'.

⬤ Excerpt from Dawna Markova, *I Will Not Die an Unlived Life: reclaiming purpose and passion*, Red Wheel/Weiser, 2000. Reproduced with permission of Dr Dawna Markova (smartwired.org).

Dawna Markova (1942–) is internationally known for her groundbreaking research on perception and learning.

○○○

FATHER
CHRIS RILEY, SDB, AM

Father Chris is founder and chief executive officer of Youth Off the Streets, which provides a range of services to young people. He has worked with disadvantaged young people for over thirty years in various roles, including teacher, youth worker, probation officer, residential carer and principal.

I believe in the sun, even when it isn't shining,
I believe in love, even when I do not feel it, and
I believe in God, even when he is silent.

Anonymous

Reflections

This was found scribbled on the wall of a concentration camp in Germany during the Second World War. We don't know who wrote it. I share this prayer with hundreds of people as it speaks of a rich hope amid life's greatest adversity. I am sure the author of this prayer would have soon faced death – yet even in such tragic circumstances, they were able to write these words.

⬤ Father Chris Riley also chose the 'Prayer of St Francis' (see page 43).

THE REVEREND DOCTOR
IAN ROBINSON

Ordained a minister in 1982. Ian works with the Uniting Church in Mount Pleasant, Western Australia. His current focus is fostering a revitalised 'church for the community'. He leads groups on retreat deep into the deserts of Australia (desertjourneys.com) in order to listen to the land and its peoples.

> My Lord God, I have no idea where I am going. I do not see the road ahead of me.
>
> I cannot know for certain where it will end.
>
> Nor do I really know myself, and the fact that I think I am following your will does not mean I am actually doing so.
>
> But I believe that the desire to please you does in fact please you. And I hope I have the desire in all that I am doing. I hope that I will never do anything apart from that desire. And I know that if I do this you will lead me by the right road, though I may know nothing about it.
>
> Therefore I will trust you always though I may seem to be lost and in the shadow of death.
>
> I will not fear, for you are ever with me, and you will never leave me to face my perils alone.
>
> Thomas Merton

Reflections

I am often confused by the options set before me, the competing voices, the dissembling promises, and I know that I can be a source of confusion, too. Somehow, the things that are too hard for me in these times of change are not too hard for God. So rich is his presence and promise in my life that I will trust him to carry me along the stream of history whether I understand what's going on or not.

Excerpt from Thomas Merton, *Thoughts in Solitude*, Abbey of Our Lady of Gethsemani, United States, 1977. Curtis Brown, NY. Used with permission.

Thomas Merton (1915–68) was a highly regarded Trappist monk and spiritual writer. He authored more than seventy books on prayer, social justice, peace and war, literature, ecumenism, monastic renewal as well as personal journals and letters.

HEATHER ROSE

Heather is the author of two novels, *White Heart* and *The Butterfly Man*. She won the 2006 Davitt Award for Crime Fiction Novel of the Year. Heather lives in Tasmania with her husband, musician Rowan Smith, and their three children.

> O Tunkashila, Wakan Tanka, Tatiya Topa, Unci Maka, Wapila, Wapila ...
>
> **Lakota (Native American) Prayer**

Reflections

In the mornings I like to climb the hill behind our house to watch the sunrise and these are always my first words. I learned this prayer as a young woman when I travelled to the United States for four years to participate in Lakota ceremonies. The Lakota are one of the seven tribes of the great Sioux Nation, whose lands were the plains of America's mid-west.

The words say, 'Grandfather, Great Spirit, the four directions of East, West, North and South, Mother Earth, thank you with deepest gratitude.' I particularly love the word *wapila*. In Lakota it means 'to be thankful' but with great generosity. To me it means I give myself completely to life in gratitude for my life.

○○○

DOCTOR
NOURIA SULTANA SALEHI, OAM

Born in Afghanistan, Nouria studied in France then migrated to Australia. A senior scientist at the Department of Nuclear Medicine in the Royal Melbourne Hospital, Nouria is also a patron of A Just Australia – Australians for Just Refugee Programs, founder of the Afghan Support Group, Victoria, and president of Afghan Australian Volunteers Association.

> In the name of Allah, Most Gracious, Most Merciful.
> Praise be to Allah, the Cherisher and Sustainer
> of the worlds;
> Most Gracious, Most Merciful;
> Master of the Day of Judgment.
> Thee do we worship, and Thine aid we seek.
> Show us the straight way,
> The way of those on whom Thou hast bestowed Thy
> Grace, those whose (portion) is not wrath, and who go
> not astray.
>
> Qur'an 1:1-7

Reflections

This surah (chapter), Al-Fatiha was the first complete surah revealed to the prophet. This surah is known as 'Seven oft-repeated verses'. It is also called 'Mother of book', the foundation and essence of the Holy Qur'an. Its recitation is mandatory in each Islamic prayer. It is recited at least seventeen times daily in the five obligatory prayers. This prayer is taught by Allah (Almighty God) himself to humankind as a favour, to let them know the format of prayer acceptable to him. This prayer is for all who want to study his message. It is placed at the very beginning to teach readers that to sincerely benefit from the Qur'an, they should offer this prayer to the *Rabb* (Lord) of the universe.

I sincerely believe that Al-Fatiha is the prayer, of the believer, and the rest of the Qur'an is the answer from Allah. The believer prays to Allah to be shown the 'right way' and Allah places the whole of the Qur'an before the believer in answer to his or her prayer, as if to say: 'This is the guidance that you have asked for.'

Qur'an 1:1–7, the Opening of the Qur'an (surah al-Fatiha), translated by Abdullah Yusuf Ali, 1934.
This prayer was also chosen by Zuleyha Keskin (see her entry on page 101) who writes this observation:

ZULEYHA KESKIN

This prayer describes to me my creator, reminding me that my God is a merciful God. I also like the way it talks about the straight path because this is my purpose in life. For me, this is achieved by living a balanced life, and having a good understanding of my purpose in life and thus my creator. Also, it mentions this world and the hereafter, reminding me that this life is only part of my overall journey, which helps me to put things in perspective.

○○○

THE MOST REVEREND METROPOLITAN ARCHBISHOP
PAUL SALIBA

Lebanese-born, Paul is Metropolitan Archbishop for Australia and New Zealand. Moving to United States, he augmented his theology studies with a doctorate in history – while restoring attendance at the church to which he was assigned. Later, as parish priest of Washington DC, he focused on drug and alcohol problems.

Have mercy upon me, O God,
According to your loving kindness;
According to the multitude of your tender mercies,
Blot out my transgressions.
Wash me thoroughly from my iniquity,
And cleanse me from my sin.

Psalm 51:1-3 New King James Bible

Reflections

The prayer is coming from a pious and repentant heart and meets the requirements of prayer, which include request, thanksgiving and glorification.

CHRIS SARRA

Chris has been involved in Indigenous education as a researcher, teacher, guidance counsellor and lecturer. Since 1998 when he became principal at Cherbourg State School in Queensland, attendance rates and literacy and numeracy have improved. Following this, community expectations of what Indigenous children can achieve have lifted.

> The greatest achievement was at first and for time a dream.
> The oak sleeps in the acorn. The bird waits in the egg.
> And in the highest vision of a soul, a waking angel stirs.
> Dreams are the seedlings of realities.
>
> James Allen

Reflections

I came across this passage many years ago; and it resonated so strongly with me as a young Aboriginal man living in a society that really stifled our true capacity by bombarding us with negative and limited perceptions of who we are. Unfortunately this stereotype persists from many angles today and many young Indigenous people continue to be deceived into subscribing to this negative perception, thinking that being Aboriginal is somehow about being at the bottom.

My message to young Aboriginal people today is that given the ancient connection that only we have to our land, and whether we or other people around us believe this or not, tremendous power and strength exists within us. I know this is true because dreams really have been the seedlings of my amazing realities.

● James Allen (1864–1912) was a nineteenth-century English writer. His best-known work was the classic self-help book *As a Man Thinketh*, first published in 1902.

PETER SCULTHORPE, AO, OBE

One of Australia's pre-eminent composers, Peter began writing music at an early age, and when he was thirteen years old decided to make a career in music. For many years he lectured at Sydney University, where he is now an emeritus professor. Peter's portrait by artist Eric Smith won the 1982 Archibald Prize.

> I know that we degrade the land and pollute the air. We destroy the past and deny the future. We're told that by the middle of this ... century the world's population will have doubled itself. In spite of all that faces us ... I feel today that I'm morally bound to attempt to write music that uplifts the human spirit.
>
> Peter Sculthorpe

Reflections

At the risk of seeming immodest, I have quoted from my autobiography. Apart from global warming, my greatest fear is world population growth, with its attendant increase in human hatred. So everyday, I aspire to uplift others. If I can achieve this, perhaps I can inspire others to do the same.

Excerpt from Peter Sculthorpe, *Sun Music: journeys and reflections from a composer's life*, ABC Books, Sydney, Australia, 1999.

FRANCES SEEN, OAM

Frances has lived in Beaconsfield, Tasmania for fifty-six years, and is a community minister with the Uniting Church. When two miners were trapped underground in Beaconsfield for two weeks in 2006, the church was open twenty-four hours a day for the many individuals who felt moved to pray.

Be positive

The secret of making something work is believing,
Then to hold that clear, definite vision in your mind
And see it working out step by step,
Without thought of doubt or disbelief,
You can make it happen.

Author unknown

Reflections

This verse was on a pocket inspiration that was given to me on 26 April 2006. It remained in my pocket every day throughout the events surrounding the recovery of two miners trapped in Beaconsfield Mine. The card was only removed from my jacket on 17 October 2006 when the garment was washed. Without being fully aware of its impact for our prayer warriors, I give thanks to God for the person who gave this verse to me.

 Frances also chose the Lord's Prayer (see page 46).

○○○

KURANDA SEYFETTIN SEYIT

Kuranda was born in Turkey and holds a masters degree in peace and conflict studies from the University of Sydney. He is founder and director of FAIR (the Forum on Australia's Islamic Relations), a community relations and advocacy group which in 2004 was a co-recipient in the National Multicultural Marketing Awards for their work in the Goodness and Kindness Project. He is a documentary filmwriter and director and in 2003 Kuranda was selected by *The Bulletin Magazine* amongst the Smart 100 Australians in the category of Society.

> The breeze at dawn has secrets to tell you.
> Don't go back to sleep.
> You must ask for what you really want.
> Don't go back to sleep.
> People are going back and forth across the doorsill
> where the two worlds touch.
> The door is round and open.
> Don't go back to sleep.
>
> Mawlana Jalalud'din Rumi

Reflections

This is one of my favourite Sufi reflections as it reminds me that we are like the breeze or the *nafis* (Arabic): the breath within us that regulates life and on which the divine message is carried.

I believe that we must seize the day and not allow ourselves to rest, lest we miss an opportunity to please Allah. Although sleep is nourishing and desirous, we should metaphorically stay awake and raise our God-consciousness. God willing.

⬤ Excerpt from Mawlana Jalalud'din Rumi, 'Chapter 4 – Spring Giddiness', in *The Essential Rumi*, translated by Coleman Barks with John Moyne, AJ Arberry and Reynold Nicholson, HarperCollins, New York, 1996. Used with permission.

Mawlana Jalalud'din Rumi (1207–73CE) was a revered mystical Sufi poet, as well as a jurist, theologian and teacher of Sufism.

○○○

RUTH SHATFORD, AM

After a long career in education, including two decades as principal of Tara Anglican School for Girls, Ruth is now in early retirement. She is active in the Anglican Church and operates a small travel agency which specialises in custom-designed, independent trips to France.

> O thou, to whom to love and to be are one,
> hear my faith – cry for them who are more
> thine than mine.
> Give each of them what is best for each.
> I cannot tell what it is.
> But thou knowest.
> I only ask thou love them and keep them
> with the loving and keeping
> thou didst show to Mary's Son and thine.
>
> Alistair MacLean

Reflections

As a school principal, I was happy to be reminded of the preciousness to God of individuals, and of my need to constantly commend them to him because of my lack of confidence that I should know what was best for them. It was a relief to be assured that his 'loving and keeping' shown to his Son would also be shown to the students, and that in Jesus, he shares our humanity.

Alistair MacLean, 'Blessing for the Children', in *The Little Book of Celtic Blessings*, ed. Caitlin Matthews, Element Books Ltd, Shaftesbury, UK, 1994. First published in 1937 in *Hebridean Altars*, Moray Press, Edinburgh, 1937.

Caitlin Matthews is a respected writer and teacher of Celtic traditions, shamanism, British myths and practical spirituality.

OOO

DOCTOR
GENE SHERMAN

Director and proprietor of Sherman Galleries since 1986, Gene sits on the boards of the National Gallery of Australia Foundation, the Venice Biennale Commissioner's Council and the Australia–Israel Cultural Exchange. In 2003, the French Government awarded her the *Chevalier de l'Ordre des Arts et des Lettres.*

Go placidly amid the noise and the haste,
and remember what peace there may be in silence.
As far as possible, without surrender,
be on good terms with all persons.
Speak your truth quietly and clearly;
and listen to others,
even to the dull and the ignorant;
they too have their story.

Attributed to Max Ehrmann

Reflections

Desiderata was first sent to me years ago by a revolutionary Japanese textile house.

The values I aspire to, and in terms of which I try to lead my life, are clear principles unemotionally expressed: a sensitive openness to other perspectives; bold action; change seen as growth; and appreciation for the gift of life.

I'm inspired by bridge-builders across cultural, religious, linguistic, generational and socio-economic divisions – people who refuse to label their fellow human beings and who keep dialogue going wherever possible, marking the exchange with generosity of spirit and hoping that similar generosity might be forthcoming.

I judge others only where the will to communicate – and respect for differing perspectives – is unambiguously absent. In most situations, at least on the personal level, time given to understanding context and the ability to empathise helps cross the unnecessary monumental divides that often cripple human progress.

● Excerpt from Max Ehrmann, *Desiderata*. First copyrighted by Ehrmann in 1927.
Max Ehrmann (1872–1945) was an American poet and philosopher. *Desiderata* – Latin for 'things to be desired' – is his best-known work. He is believed to have sent out *Desiderata* as part of a personal Christmas message in 1933.

PROFESSOR
PETER SINGER

Peter Singer is regarded as one of the world's most influential philosophers. He is currently professor of Bioethics at Princeton University as well as laureate professor at the Centre for Applied Philosophy and Public Ethics at the University of Melbourne. His well known books include *Animal Liberation, Practical Ethics, Rethinking Life and Death,* and *The Ethics of What We Eat.*

> I guess basically one wants to feel that one's life has amounted to more than just consuming products and generating garbage. I think that one likes to look back and say that one's done the best one can to make this a better place for others. You can look at it from this point of view: what greater motivation can there be than doing whatever one possibly can to reduce pain and suffering?
>
> Henry Spira

Reflections

My friend and fellow animal rights activist Henry Spira responded in this way when I asked him what motivated him to choose the life he had lived. He had terminal cancer and knew that he didn't have very long to live. An atheist, he was under no illusions about surviving the death of his body. But he was content with the life he had lived — more than content, in fact, fulfilled — and he was not depressed or afraid of dying. He had spent all his life siding with the oppressed — marching for civil rights in the American south, struggling for union reform in the merchant marine, where he worked for many years, then in New York City public schools teaching children from impoverished backgrounds, and eventually becoming a highly effective campaigner for animal rights. His words about the best way to live mean a lot to me.

● Henry Spira, in Peter Singer, *Ethics into Action: Henry Spira and the Animal Rights Movement*, Melbourne University Press, 1998.

MONINDER SINGH

Formerly an associate professor at Punjab Agricultural University, India, Moninder is media coordinator for the United Indian Associations and coordinator of the Punjabi Council of Australia. In 2006, Moninder and his real estate business team were the main promoters of the successful nineteenth Australian Sikh Games.

Ik Onkaar	There is only one God.
Sat Naam	His name is truth.
Karta Purkh	He is the creator.
Nir Bhau	He is without fear.
Nir Vair	He is without hate.
Akaal Moorat	He is beyond time – immortal.
Ajooni	He is beyond birth and death.
Saibhang	He is self-existent.
Gur Parsaad	He is realised by the Guru's grace.

Guru Nanak

Reflections

I have chosen the *Mool Mantar* (literally, the root verse), composed by Guru Nanak, as it sums up the basic belief of the Sikhs. The Sikh Holy Book *Guru Granth Sahib* begins with this *Mool Mantar*. Every Sikh is expected to recite it daily.

Most of the hymns in *Guru Granth*, written by the Sikh Gurus and radical saints, are prayers offered to the Lord or the Guru. A Sikh offers his prayers in the presence of *Guru Granth Sahib*, the Sikh scripture, if he can. But if he is away from home or travelling, he can offer his prayers any time, at any place.

This prayer is offered in Sikh Temples every morning and evening. The formal prayer of the Sikhs ends with the words, '*Nanak Nam Chardi Kala, Tere Bhane Sarbat Da Bhala*', which means 'the name of the Lord emanating from the Guru [Guru Nanak] may bring high spirits and the welfare of all in his will'.

● Guru Nanak, 'Mool Mantar', in *Guru Granth*.
The *Guru Granth* is the religious holy scripture of the Sikh faith. The holy text spans 1430 pages and contains the actual words spoken by the Sikh Gurus and also writings of people from other faiths, including Hinduism and Islam.

FATHER
STEVE SINN, SJ

Steve is a Jesuit priest who has worked in the Parish of Elizabeth Bay since 1993. In that time he has been involved in the work of Canice's Kitchen, a place of hospitality for street people.

> Soul of Christ, sanctify me
> Body of Christ, save me
> Blood of Christ, inebriate me
> Water from the side of Christ, wash me
> Passion of Christ, strengthen me.
> O good Jesus, hear me
> Within thy wounds, hide me
> Never let me be separated from thee
> From the wicked enemy, defend me
> At the hour of my death, call me
> And bid me come to thee
> That with thy saints I may praise thee
> For ever and ever.
>
> Amen
>
> **Attributed to Pope John XXII**

Reflections

I have said 'Anima Christi' ever since I was a boarder at Burke Hall, a preparatory school for Xavier College in Melbourne.

● 'Anima Christi' is often used after receiving the Eucharist. It originated in the fourteenth century. Its authorship is uncertain although it was possibly written by Pope John XXII (1249–1316).

OOO

THE RIGHT REVEREND
KEITH SLATER

Ordained in 1975, Keith served in the Anglican Diocese of Rockhampton and Brisbane. In 2003 he became bishop of the Diocese of Grafton. He is a professed member of the worldwide Third Order, Society of St Francis, and served as the minister general of the Order from 1999 to 2005.

> Here, and in all your churches throughout the world,
> We adore you, O Christ, and we bless you;
> Because by your holy cross, you have redeemed the world.
> Amen.
>
> The Third Order, Society of St Francis

Reflections

This prayer brings alive the recognition of God's presence everywhere, and those who believe bow in humble adoration to God.

This prayer is used by Franciscans as they enter church and is like a 'centering prayer', placing oneself open before God in Christ. It is used daily by members of the Anglican Third Order, Society of St Francis, of which I am a member. It is prayed in a form which is known as the Community Obedience and is seen as that which binds the Order together worldwide, day by day.

The things which I hold passionately are shaped by my understandings of Franciscan vocation and are summed up in the objects of the Order:

- Making Christ known and loved everywhere.
- Seeking to live simply.
- Striving to build communities of peace and harmony.

They connect with seeking to live life in a non-violent way, and with the recognition of the stewardship of creation, and especially in the present debate of human impact on climate change.

● Excerpt from 'The Community Obedience', the Third Order, Society of St Francis Manual (as used in the Australian Province).

○○○

LORD MAYOR
JOHN SO

An ex-teacher, businessman and Ethnic Affairs Commissioner, John has twice been elected as Mayor of Melbourne City Council. Born in Hong Kong, he moved to Australia aged seventeen and took a degree in Science and Education at the University of Melbourne. He is passionate about promoting Melbourne.

> Australia is one of the world's most peaceful countries; home to a welcoming multicultural community. We are learning from our past to create a bright future and we have a role to play in this new global era. We have the opportunity to consider people beyond our shores when making decisions locally, to balance our urban and natural environments, and to spread a message of peace and harmony wherever we go.
>
> John So

OOO

CHARMAINE SOLOMON, OAM

Since emigrating from Sri Lanka over forty years ago, Charmaine has become a respected authority on Asian food. Author of more than thirty books, she is a regular contributor to newspapers, magazines and television programs. Charmaine's philosophy is that all meals are acts of love and nurturing.

Dear Lord,

If only I could still the hands of time,
stop them just where they are right now,
and hold the world in a beautiful golden bubble,
a place where nothing changes.

Well, maybe some things could be better.
We'd like to have more time together
and not have to work so hard, so long,
to pay the bills and keep things going.
But I don't expect perfection.
And you have blessed us
with strength and willingness to work.
You have blessed us with children;
help us enjoy them and not only spend our time
training them, bringing them up right.
You have blessed us with love for each other;
after all these years there is still
the fun of jokes shared,
the benediction of tenderness,
the flame of desire.

Yes, Lord, I love my life.
I thank you for this gift that embraces all gifts.
Take from me the fear of change,
give me faith to believe not only with my head
but with my heart
that your mercies are from everlasting to everlasting.

continued overleaf

May I let the clock of life move on unafraid,
knowing the time ahead is in your hands
just like the years before.

Charmaine Solomon

Reflections

Many years ago, I wrote a book called *Love and a Wooden Spoon* – a collection of stories about the life I share with my loved ones, featuring recipes we use often and some poems which I had written about the homely, everyday things which make life worth living. 'Today and Tomorrow' was written when I was a young wife and mother. Now my husband and I have been married almost 50 years, and if there is one thing I know, it is that change is inevitable. However, this was written from my heart and therefore I feel it is still valid to share.

● Charmaine Solomon, 'Today and Tomorrow', in *Love and a Wooden Spoon*, Hill of Content, © Charmaine Solomon, 1981.

NAOMI STEER

Naomi is a human rights lawyer and the founding National Director of 'Australia for UNHCR', an international aid organisation that raises funds to support the UN Refugee Agency's humanitarian and emergency relief work. She has visited many refugee camps and is continually inspired by the courage and hope that refugees maintain despite often desperate circumstances.

> I have experienced first hand, as an eight year old girl, what it is like to be saved by UNHCR, to be given food or shelter when you are driven from your home and family. Now I want my voice to keep alive the plight of the refugees still in the camps so they are not forgotten. No one wants to be a refugee, they just want to live a normal life like everyone else but they are powerless to change the situation in their country, or to change their circumstances.
>
> Adut Dau Atem

Reflections

As a young Sudanese girl of eight, Adut Dau Atem (see entry on page 11) lost everything. Forced to flee her country she walked across Africa for two years with other 'lost children of Sudan' before finding refuge in a camp from where she was eventually resettled in Australia.

When Sophie Weldon (see entry on page 186) wrote about Adut in the UNHCR's 2003 writing competition, no-one foresaw the impact. Adut's story featured widely in the media and was used to promote understanding about refugees. When people ask me what they can do to help, I use Sophie and Adut as my inspiration. Adut says, 'refugees are powerless to change their situation', but we are not.

Since meeting Adut, Sophie and her family, friends and local community have worked to reunite Adut with family members still in camps in Sudan. They also decided to try and find Adut's mother, believed dead. After an extraordinary search, Adut's mother was found and was able to come to Australia to be reunited with family after more than ten years.

Sophie and Adut are both Special Youth Representatives for Australia for UNHCR.

● Adut Dau Atem, speech given at the UNHCR World Refugee Day Breakfast, 17 June 2005, Westin Hotel, Sydney.

JAMES STRONG, AO

Renowned businessman and arts philantropist, James Strong is chairman of Woolworths, Insurance Australia Group, Rip Curl Group and the Australia Council for Arts. He is also a director of Qantas Airways Ltd. Among the many awards James has received for his achievements is the Smithsonian Institute's Laureate Hall of Fame Award for Commercial Air Transport.

Always treat others as you would like to be treated.

A modern expression of The Golden Rule.

Reflections

This was a standard set and consistently observed by my father, who supervised a large workforce in an abattoir. He was a successful leader who treated everyone with respect, and as individuals.

 A moral principle common to many religions.

OOO

ARCHBISHOP STYLIANOS

Primate of the Greek Orthodox Archdiocese of Australia, Archbishop Stylianos has studied theology in Turkey and in Germany, and became associate professor of systematic theology at the University of Thessalonika in Greece. He has been honoured for his contribution to European cultural achievements. A renowned poet, Archbishop Stylianos was given the Award for Poetry from the Academy of Athens in 1980. Currently he is dean of St Andrew's Greek Orthodox Theological College, Sydney.

The other is ineffable
neither small nor large
an anonymous yearning
regardless of how familiar or distant
he is my nearest god.

However different the other
much more astonishing
is my Lord and God
only in touching him
am I ecstatically redeemed
in the fulfilment of this world.

Archbishop Stylianos

Reflections

This poem is a kind of hymn for every person created in the image and likeness of God.

● Archbishop Stylianos, 'The Other', May 1976.

○○○

SINNA SUNDARAM

Sri Lankan-born Sinna worked in Singapore as a management consultant then migrated to Australia in the 1980s. He is the director of finance at Sutherland Hospital in New South Wales. Sinna has spent a substantial part of his life in Australia helping to build a Hindu temple in Westmead, Sydney.

> Om bhoor-bhuvah-svah
> Tat savitur varenyam
> Bhargo devasya dheemahi
> Dhiyo yo nah prachodayaat.
>
> O God! you are the giver of life,
> The remover of pains and sorrows,
> The bestower of happiness,
> O Creator of the universe,
> May we receive your supreme light which will destroy all sins.
> May you guide our intellect in the right direction.
>
> Gayathri Mantra

Reflections

The 'Gayathri Mantra' is recited many times by priests in Hindu temples and also used by ordinary people. If correctly pronounced and prayed in deep contemplation, its sound alone is beautiful and is said to have beneficial effects on the person chanting it. The prayer appeals to the highest wisdom and to brilliant cosmic energy, to make us understand our true nature. The appeal requests that we become receptive to divine wisdom and understand our very self.

Dr Pranav Pandiya, who runs a spiritual and medical facility in the Himalayas, said on a recent visit to Australia that this prayer is broadcast regularly over the intercom in his hospital and helps cardiac patients to recover with tremendous speed.

● The 'Gayathri Mantra' is a highly revered mantra from the Vedas which is one of the most ancient Hindu religious texts still in existence. It consists of fourteen words, each of which holds an important meaning.

SIMON TEDESCHI

At nine years of age Simon performed a Mozart piano concerto at the Sydney Opera House. He won his first international competition when he was thirteen years old, and has since matured into one of Australia's most recognisable and established pianists. Acclaimed harmonica virtuoso Larry Adler said Simon 'reminds me of a young Rachmaninoff'.

Tyger, Tyger, burning bright
In the forest of the night,
What immortal hand or eye
Could frame thy fearful symmetry?

In what distant deeps or skies
Burnt the fire of thine eyes?
On what wings dare he aspire?
What the hand dare seize the fire?

And what shoulder and what art
Could twist the sinews of thy heart?
And when thy heart began to beat,
What dread hand and what dread feet?

What the hammer? What the chain?
In what furnace was thy brain?
What the anvil? What dread grasp
Dare its deadly terrors clasp?

When the stars threw down their spears,
And water'd heaven with their tears,
Did he smile his work to see?
Did he who made the lamb make thee?

Tyger, Tyger, burning bright
In the forests of the night,
What immortal hand or eye
Dare frame thy fearful symmetry?

William Blake

Reflections

It really reminds me of my childhood. Not only do I remember my parents reading this to me, but I also remember studying it in school. It has such emotive power and imagery; it doesn't need music, the words alone have such impact.

🔵 William Blake, 'The Tyger', from the collection, 'Songs of Experience', in Songs of Innocence and of Experience. First published in 1794. William Blake (1757–1827) was a British poet, painter, visionary mystic and engraver.

OOO

CHARLES 'BUD' TINGWELL, AM

Born in Coogee, New South Wales, Bud served as a pilot in the RAAF during the Second World War. An actor who has worked in many radio, theatre, film and television productions, his best-known films are *Innocence*, *The Castle* and *Irresistible*. Bud's reflection below is his long-held belief.

Sunday school at St Nicholas Church of England, as it then was, in Coogee was a vaguely pleasant memory. Impressions were that Jesus must have been a good bloke to know and that he said some wise things, especially on a mountain near Galilee. Or was it just a hill? The thought of 'turning the other cheek' and not seeking revenge appealed to me. I naively thought if world leaders obeyed those rules that war, in which my father was so badly wounded, would never happen again.

But revenge was sought, and cheeks never seemed to be turned for a very long time. Until Nelson Mandela was released from gaol.

I expected violent chaos to be the result. I was wrong. Negotiations, discussions, agreements all seemed to provide for a troubled but generally peaceful country. As President of South Africa, Mandela provided inspiration for millions of people around the world. He also provided me with the belief that what was said on the mountain or hill 2000 years ago was a pretty good idea. It could save the planet we are so privileged to inhabit.

Bud Tingwell

DOCTOR
JOHN TOOTH, OAM

John is internationally renowned for his work with dementia patients, particularly at Adards Nursing Home in Hobart, Tasmania. In the 1960s, he also established in Goulburn, NSW, Australia's first community-sponsored half-way house for the mentally ill and later was appointed medical commissioner of Tasmanian Mental Health Services Commission. John lectures in dementia management and design.

> There is an anecdote, which is probably apocryphal, about Bertrand Russell in a London taxi. The taxi driver, when he found out who he was driving, said excitedly 'Bertrand Russell! Now, Gov, I have always wanted to know from the likes of you, what's life all about then?'
>
> After a moment of reflection Russell said, 'It is all about man's continual search for Beauty, Goodness and Truth.'
>
> Unattributed

Reflections

Over the years I have often thought of these words and how they might fit in with the tenets of the Christian faith in which I was brought up. As I learnt more about other religions I realised that the search for 'goodness' and 'truth' was inherent in all those I studied. A search for 'beauty' is usually not apparent!

For myself, beauty has been important. I think I was about five or six years old when I was overwhelmed by the beauty of a garden in rural Sussex, England. From then on I have continually searched for beauty in gardens (preferably large ones with sweeping lawns and great trees), or landscapes of hilly country with shades of brown and green. I'm now seventy-four, and over twenty years my wife and I have created a large garden of rare beauty on the slopes of Mount Wellington in Tasmania. The sense of fulfilment is immense.

Goodness and truth have been guiding beacons from primary school days for my passage through life in work and family and social relationships; that is not to say that wrongdoing and falsity have not also crept in, but when they have there has always been a sense of shame and guilt. In my work as a psychiatrist over forty years it has been relatively easy to find avenues in which to develop goodness, and I have always had as an adjunct to this fulfilling work the joy of working with volunteers as they deliver services to the disadvantaged. It is interesting to note that I have never met a rich volunteer; there seems to be something destructive about wealth in the search for goodness.

Now I come to truth. The truths with which I have been involved are medical and scientific as well as historical, as I have been a passionate historian all my life. It has been said that half an inch of faded ink is worth more than all the anecdotage in the world in the search for truth in history. Philosophical truths are more difficult for me and I have to leave this search to people like Bertrand Russell.

KEYSAR TRAD

Lebanese-born Keysar was a public servant for fourteen years before immersing himself in community work and human rights activism. He has translated several Islamic books from Arabic to English and gives regular television, radio and newspaper interviews in relation to Islam and the Muslim community.

In the security and care of Allah, I leave you.
O Allah, bring to them all goodness and protect them
from all evil.

O Allah make good their day, guard them and protect
them, make them learn the most from their lessons, give
them success in every test, inspire them to what is right,
embellish them with the best of manners and behaviour.

(I ask Allah to) grant you refuge through His perfect
words, against all evil and to protect you from envy.

Allah! There is no god except Him, the Alive, the Eternal.
Neither slumber nor sleep overtaketh him. Unto him
belongs whatsoever is in the heavens and whatsoever is in
the earth. Who could intercede with Him except by His
leave? He knows that which is in front of them and that
which is behind them while they encompass nothing of
His knowledge except what He willed. His throne
includes the heavens and the earth, and He is never weary
of preserving them. He is the Sublime, the Tremendous.

Attributed to Keysar Trad

Reflections

I have nine children. I recite these prayers for each of the school-aged children every day as I drop them off to school. The purpose of these prayers is to invoke the protection, compassion and love of Allah.

⬤ Keysar Trad incorporated short prayers based on verses from the Qur'an, including Qur'an 2:255, translated by Muhammad Marmaduke Pickthall, 1930.

TOM UREN, AO

After an early career as a professional boxer, Tom was a Federal Labor MP from 1958 to 1990. He was the last veteran of the Second World War in the House of Representatives. Tom has campaigned for various causes, especially the environment, refugees, peace and social justice.

The strong should look after the weak,
The young look after the not so young,
The fit look after the sick.
We should collectivise a substantial portion of our income
to help protect our sick, and needy people.
We need to seek a more tolerant world.
We should defend our human and civil rights,
wherever they are violated.
Oppose violence at a personal, national and international
level.
Oppose war as the solution to our international problems.
Protect, enhance and rehabilitate our environment.
If we destroy it, we are destroying a part of ourselves.
Recognise that we are interrelated.
Australians should recognise we are part of our planet.
Why is it in time of crisis – we need each other?
Why, in normal times, why can't we be more collective?
We should build friendship and understanding between
people and nations.

Tom Uren

Reflections

When a Japanese student asked me about my philosophy, I outlined my experience of the collective spirit serving under Colonel 'Weary' Dunlop on the Burma Thailand Railway during the Second World War. On further reflection, I wrote the above.

Life is my educator: I've drawn from people. I get on ferries packed with overseas visitors coming or going to Darling Harbour and I strike up discussions with them. I talk with everybody. That's the way you learn. I've always mixed with people from a broad base.

I've drawn from men and women of goodwill all my life: people like Mahatma Gandhi, Pope John XXIII, Martin Luther King, Franklin D. Roosevelt and Mary MacKillop. Others like Paul Robeson and Ho Chi Minh and my old mate Jim Cairns had an influence on me too. I was moved by Paulo Freire's book, *The Pedagogy of the Oppressed*, and his attitude of love for your fellow human being. The argument is that if you are a revolutionary, you do it because you want to make the world more equitable, just, free and open and that's what I've fought for all my life.

I think the future of politics and the future of leadership lies with women. More and more it's the women, particularly the younger ones, who are coming through with greater leadership and that's where the hope is for a better world. They're not so competitive. I'm a competitor but I am also a collectivist. You can't always win and, in fact, sometimes when you are defeated you become a better person. You gain a bit more humility.

I have moved away from the Christian faith yet I am often moved by Christ's stories of compassion in the New Testament, and I've wept on many occasions when reading them. But when I made the decision to step across the line towards a non-believer's position, I was left with a humanist perspective of life.

OOO

ADRIAN VANAS

During the Second World War Adrian and his wife, Bertha, joined the Dutch 'underground' movement. A government employee, he was put in charge of food distribution at Westerbork, Holland's largest Nazi transit camp. He secretly removed names from deportation lists, supplied false papers and found safe houses, saving nearly 1000 lives. They were honoured with the *Righteous Among the Nations* Award.

Hear a just cause, O Lord! Attend to my cry. Give ear to my prayer. I have avoided the ways of the violent. My steps have held fast to your path. You are my rock in whom I take refuge. Why is there so much suffering? Why are people moving away from you? Show the world that you are having this world in your hands. In my distress I call upon you. I cry for help, let the people become aware that You are the mighty one,

The only one! You have chosen yourself a people, a nation. You are bringing them home according to your promises. You left your land barren for nearly 2000 years. You reshaped that land in 1948 and made it once again a land of milk and honey in which your people may live in peace. You are fulfilling your promises by bringing your people home. Give them that right to live in peace. Make an end to their sufferings. Restore the fortunes of your people. The fool says in his heart, 'There is no God'. They are corrupt, they do abominable deeds, they have gone astray. They are in great terror. They slander with their tongues and do evil to their friends. Make them aware that you will never come back on a once-given promise. Open their eyes, Lord, so that they may see to love their neighbour instead of hating him,

Amen.

Attributed to Adrian Vanas

Reflections

Mine is a wonderful guided life. I thought I could direct my life the way I liked, but I came to the conclusion that the Lord had other plans. Then, I did not understand why – but looking back I can see the reasons now. If I had followed my own way, I would have been stranded. My story has been recorded in books and documentaries in Dutch, and in newspapers all over the world.

I see life as something that has not happened by accident. Each and every one of us is born to fulfil a certain task, major or minor.

◗ Adrian Vanas' personal reflections are based on Psalms 14, 15, 17 and 18.

○○○

SABINA VAN DER LINDEN

Sabina's parents, brother, grandparents and all other relatives were killed by the Nazis. Fostered by many kind and courageous people, she survived the Holocaust, married, and emigrated to Australia. Via her involvement in Living Historian Programs and Courage to Care, Sabina works towards communal tolerance and harmony.

Dear God,

It is I, the elephant,
your creature,
who is talking to you.
I am so embarrassed by my great self,
and truly it is not my fault
if I spoil your jungle a little with my big feet.
Let me be careful and behave wisely,
always keeping my dignity and poise.
Give me such philosophic thought,
that I can rejoice everywhere I go,
in the loveable oddity of things.

Amen.

Carmen Bernos de Gasztold

Reflections

I just love this poem. I also chose the St Francis peace prayer because it expresses so beautifully my hopes and aspirations not to be a bystander, but to raise awareness and to make a contribution for our world to be a better place to live.

'I have learned from my bitter experience that hatred begets hatred. I have learned that we must not remain silent and that each of us as an individual must fight the evil of racism, discrimination, prejudice, inhumanity. I have repeatedly said that I do not believe in the collective guilt'. Quote from Sabina's speech at the inauguration of the Memorial to the Murdered Jews of Europe in Berlin in 2005.

Carmen Bernos de Gasztold, 'The Prayer of the Elephant', in *Prayers from the Ark*, translated by Rumer Godden, Viking, 1992. Reproduced with permission of Curtis Brown Group Ltd, London, on behalf of The Estate of Rumer Godden. © Rumer Godden, 1947. Carmen Bernos de Gasztold (1919–), a reclusive French author, lived in a Benedictine Abbey after the Second World War. *Prayers from the Ark*, her most famous book, is a selection of prayers by some of the animals in Noah's Ark.

Sabina also chose the *Prayer of St Francis* (see page 45)

○○○

NANCY BIRD-WALTON, AO, OBE

In 1935, Nancy became the youngest commercial and professionally licensed female pilot in the British Commonwealth. Known as the 'Angel of the Outback' for her work with the Far West Children's Health Scheme, in 1950 she founded the Australian Women Pilots Association.

> **Whatever you can do or dream, begin it.**
>
> Attributed to Johann Wolfgang von Goethe

Reflections

This is what my mother taught me when I was growing up and I have applied this philosophy in my daily life. I also learnt good manners, consideration for others and an appreciation of good music and religion from my dear mother; to her these were natural attributes.

Johann Wolfgang von Goethe (1749–1832), a giant of literature, was a celebrated German poet, playwright, novelist and scientist. Nancy also chose 'Always treat others as you would like to be treated.' (see page 172)

DOCTOR
GUY WARREN, OAM

Guy is an Australian painter, printmaker and art educator. His works are found in major international galleries, the National Gallery of Australia, all Australian state and many regional art galleries. He is represented in institutional, corporate and private collections in Australia and abroad. Guy won the Archibald Prize in 1985.

Throughout a lifetime of eighty-six years, many things happen and many ideas surface. It is difficult to identify prayers that were particularly significant – more difficult still to identify particular prayers or reflections. However, two experiences do stand out for me.

The first happened during the Second World War, when I was a young soldier on the island of Bougainville, New Guinea. I made many drawings of the landscape and the local people and was fascinated by the way these people unselfconsciously decorated their bodies. Given the highly decorative and textured nature of the landscape in which they lived, it seemed to comment on the relationship between humankind and the environment, and suggest a powerful metaphor for the interdependence between them. This simple idea has been reinforced many times since for me by other people and other experiences (such as James Lovelock's books on the Gaia hypothesis) and has inspired many of the paintings I have produced.

The second experience involves the Australian landscape painter Lloyd Rees, a friend and colleague, and a man of great wisdom, compassion and understanding. Some years before his death, he turned to me one day and said suddenly, 'Isn't it wonderful, Guy, to think of ourselves as being here in the middle of eternity?' What a cosmic, inspirational thought! Our day-to-day worries and concerns about our 'three score years and ten' – or whatever one may be lucky enough to have – seemed suddenly insignificant. It put everything into perspective. I remind myself of it constantly.

Guy Warren

SOPHIE WELDON

When she was fourteen years old, Sophie Weldon's desire to record at first hand the story of a young refugee resulted in a life-changing encounter with Adut Dau Atem (see her entry on page 11). Their friendship grew, and the two young women have worked extensively to raise awareness about the plight of the world's seventeen million refugees.

> The kind of hope that I often think about ... I understand
> above all as a state of mind, not a state of the world.
> Either we have hope within us or we don't; it is a
> dimension of the soul, and it's not essentially dependent
> on some particular observation of the world or estimate of
> the situation ... [Hope] is not the conviction that
> everything will turn out well, but the certainty that
> something makes sense, regardless of how it turns out.
>
> Václav Havel

Reflections

I grew up in a house nestled in the treetops in Sydney's northern beaches surrounded by beauty and love, salty air, warm sunshine, loud music, good books and movies, long talks in the car with Mum and long walks on the beach. My grandfather inspired me to be passionate, pursue my interests and stand up for what I believe in. He taught me that 'a dream can't become reality by just sitting around and thinking about it, go out there and give it a go', and to remember 'a failure is a failure is a failure is a success'. My mum raised my brother and me in a creative, supportive and inspiring environment.

In primary school I was taught how to get up in front of an assembly of people and motivate them to act on an idea. I wanted to make a difference but I didn't know how to start. I met Adut when I was fourteen years old, in the prime of my teenage angst. Her story and her quiet resolve affected me so profoundly that my whole perspective of the world and my place in it changed.

When I met Adut I didn't know what to expect. By the end of the interview I was staggered by the depth of Adut's story and the strength of her spirit. How could I relate to any of this? At the time I was having troubles at school with friends. After hearing of someone's life filled with such loss, such pain, such hardship, I felt I was stupid to be worrying about the things in my life which suddenly didn't seem so important: it ceased to be a refugee issue; it was actually someone's life.

Adut had been through situations of life and death survival when I was learning to ride a bike. When I looked into her eyes it was hard to believe that this girl not much older than me still had so much grace and gentleness after everything she had been through. For me, the emotional experience was very hard to handle that night and Adut could see this. She leant over to me and said, 'Sophie, this is not your fault. What happened to me is not your fault.'

In that moment I understood that I was powerless to have any impact on Adut's past but I could share my good life with her and together we could look to the future. It helped her to have someone just listening to her story. Since the moment I met Adut and recorded our interview my life changed … I didn't just write about her story, *I became a part of her story*. The friendship I have forged with Adut and the impact she has had, not only on me but my family and school community, is something that will stay with me forever.

My mum read me the quotation from Fritjof Capra's book when I was confused and troubled as I neared the end of writing Adut's story. These words by Václav Havel helped me discover a new meaning of 'hope' that I was trying to come to grips with when I was listening to Adut's story … I could sense it but it wasn't in its usual clean, blindly optimistic form. It was woven in between the deep sadness and struggle and Havel's words helped me reconcile it. Hope was there, hidden in Adut's smile, her gentleness, her resolve, her passion, and in the paradox of our own connection from such different backgrounds; in our friendship, our conversation, our sharing, our hugs, our purpose, our shared vision. It was understanding that hope and sadness can somehow exist together and can live inside you. That personal struggle can somehow be turned around and become hope and a sense of purpose.

Any type of friendship brings with it a sense of hope and Adut and I are no exception. So now Adut and I, twenty-two and eighteen years old, are continuing our journey with UNHCR, educating and supporting fundraising activities. Here we are, part of a much bigger story that now includes you as you read this book. This then is the real hope.

● Excerpt from Václav Havel, as quoted in Fritjof Capra, *The Hidden Connections: integrating the biological, cognitive and social dimensions of life into a science of sustainability*, Flamingo, London, 2003.

Václav Havel (1936–) is a Czech playwright and first president of Czech Republic.

Austrian-born, and American-based, Fritjof Capra (1939–) is a physicist and systems theorist and founding director of the Center for Ecoliteracy in Berkeley, California.

See also Naomi Steer's contribution on this friendship on page 180.

DOCTOR
MARY WESTBROOK, AM

Mary is a fellow of the Australian Psychological Society and a conjoint associate professor at the Centre for Clinical Governance Research in the Faculty of Medicine at the University of New South Wales. She uses a wheelchair, the delayed result of childhood polio. She is involved with post-polio organisations worldwide. Mary is a Quaker.

Most Noble Contessina,

... I am your friend, and my love for you goes deep. There is nothing I can give you which you have not got; but there is much, very much, that while I cannot give it, you can take. No heaven can come to us unless we rest our hearts in today. Take heaven! No peace lies in the future which is not hidden in this present little instant. Take peace!

The gloom of the world is but a shadow. Behind it, yet within our reach is joy. There is radiance and glory in the darkness, could we but see; and to see, we have only to look. Contessina, I beseech you to look.

Life is so generous a giver, but we, judging its gifts by their covering, cast them away as ugly or heavy or hard. Remove the covering and you will find beneath it a living splendour, woven by love, by wisdom, with power. Welcome it, grasp it, and you will touch the angel's hand that brings it to you. Everything we call a trial, a sorrow, or a duty, believe me, that angel's hand is there: the gift is there, and the wonder of an overshadowing presence. Our joys, too; be not content with them as joys, they too conceal diviner gifts.

Life is so full of meaning and of purpose, so full of beauty – beneath its covering – that you may find that earth but cloaks your heaven. Courage, then to claim it: that is all!

But courage you have; and the knowledge that we are pilgrims together, wending through unknown country, home.

And so this Christmas time, I greet you; not quite as the world sends greetings, but with profound esteem, and with the prayer that for you, now and forever, the day breaks and the shadows flee away ...

Attributed to Friar (Fra) Giovanni Giocondo

Reflections

The recipient of this letter, the Contessina, is thought to have suffered a bereavement and the friar anticipates that Christmas festivities and the future will be difficult times for her. I came across this letter after the long and terrible dying of John, my husband of forty-one years. It 'spoke to my condition' as I faced relearning how to live, alone, in a different world. I have returned to the letter many times as it gives me a sense of hope and purpose in attempting to contribute to a more loving and peaceful world.

 Excerpt from a letter by Friar Giovanni Giocondo. The letter's recipient is thought to have been Contessina Allagia degli Aldobrandeschi, who received it on Christmas Eve, 1513.

Friar Giovanni Giocondo (*c.* 1435–1515) was an Italian architect and classical scholar.

◯◯◯

MICHAEL WHELAN, SM

Michael is a Marist priest and is the director of Aquinas Academy Adult Education Centre in Sydney. He co-founded Catalyst for Renewal, a group seeking to promote conversation within the Catholic Church and beyond, and Spirituality in the Pub, another forum for conversation.

Once again, let me say I appreciate the loyalty of so many old friends and the interest of new ones. I shall continue to feel bound to all of you in the silence of prayer. Our real journey in life is interior: it is a matter of growth, deepening, and of an ever greater surrender to the creative action of love and grace in our hearts. Never was it more necessary for us to respond to that action. I pray we may all do so generously. God bless you.

Thomas Merton

Reflections

Thomas Merton was an amazing man, refreshing in his honesty, inspiring in his conscientious dedication to that 'real journey', and most insightful about the things that matter in the end. He loved people and cared deeply about his friends. The more I learn of Merton and read his writings the more I find myself in the presence of the 'mystery'. So much else falls into place – or out of place, as the case may be – in that context. In this brief and simple statement Merton reminds us of where our best energies should go. He calls us to account, challenges us and gives us great hope.

Excerpt from Thomas Merton, *The Road to Joy: letters of Thomas Merton to new and old friends*, selected and edited by Robert E Daggy, Copyright ©1989 by the Merton Legacy Trust. Reprinted by permission of Farrar, Straus and Giroux.
Thomas Merton (1915–1968) was a highly regarded Trappist monk and spiritual writer. He authored more than seventy books on prayer, social justice, peace and war, literature, ecumenism, monastic renewal as well as personal journals and letters.

OOO

ALI WHITE

While teaching Middle East politics at Australian universities, dialogue with his Muslim students led to Ali's conversion to Islam in 2002. He coordinates Muslims For Peace, an initiative which strives for peace with justice and stands against all oppression and injustice, 'for Allah loves the equitable' (Qur'an, 60:8–9).

> Say: He is Allah, the One!
> Allah, the eternally Besought of all!
> He begetteth not nor was begotten
> And there is none comparable unto Him.
>
> Qur'an 112:1–4

Reflections

Since the 'Creator is One', and everything is originated from one source, this means that all human beings are equal in relation to God and are from the same source; God belongs to no particular nation or a group. All individuals and all societies are mutually interconnected and mutually interdependent upon each other, since they are all united in the oneness of creation.

God's 'Oneness' thus provides the basis for the emergence of peace with justice. Instead of conflicts on the basis of nationality, ethnicity and factionalism, Islam counterposes a world in harmony, where we are able to live in equitable relations with each other, because each regards the other as equally one of God's creatures. Thus, we all have the ability to walk towards perfection and to strive towards peace with justice.

Qur'an 112:1–4, translated by Muhammed Marmaduke Pickthall, 1930.

RAY WILLIAMSON

General Secretary of the New South Wales Ecumenical Council from 1986 to 2006, Ray Williamson has worked in parish ministry, as a theology lecturer, and served as rector of St James Anglican Church, Morpeth. He has travelled to Palestine and Lebanon in support of local churches in their struggles for justice for the Palestinian people.

> Jesus our peace, you never abandon us. And the Holy Spirit always opens a way forward, the way which consists in casting ourselves into God as into the depths. And astonishment arises: these depths are not an abyss of darkness; they are God-fathomless depths of compassion and innocence.
>
> Brother Roger Shutz

Reflections

Throughout the years I have been in an ecumenical ministry, the Taizé community (Burgundy, France) has been a source of inspiration and encouragement. It is an ecumenical community that seeks to build reconciliation and to live its life as a 'parable of communion'. The modern ecumenical movement has developed out of the conviction that God calls us, the churches, to grow into communion with God and with each other.

However, in our present fractured communion with one another, we easily diminish God to an image that fits our denominational compartments, and that only consolidates our brokenness. This prayer of Brother Roger speaks to me of the fathomless depths of God, the mystery of God; and it is the wonder of mystery that draws us out of ourselves into communion. This conviction is my inspiration and hope.

⬤ Excerpt from Brother Roger, *Prayer for Each Day,* Ateliers et Presses de Taizé, 1997
© Ateliers et Presses de Taizé, 71250, Taizé, France.
    Brother Roger Shutz (1915–2005) founded the Taizé Christian ecumenical community in 1940.

PHILIP WILSON, DD, JCL

ARCHBISHOP OF ADELAIDE

Ordained to the priesthood in 1975, Archbishop Wilson is archbishop of Adelaide and president of the Australian Catholic Bishops Conference. He is also a prominent canon lawyer who has pioneered some robust child protection policies in South Australia.

Dearest Lord,

Teach me to be generous,
to serve you as you deserve,
to give and not to count the cost,
to fight and not to heed the wounds,
to labour and not to seek reward,
save that of knowing that I do your
holy will.

Amen.

Attributed to St Ignatius Loyola

Reflections

I discovered this prayer attributed to St Ignatius Loyola when I was thirteen years old. Through this prayer I expressed my enthusiastic youthful desire to serve Christ and Church. It still remains a cornerstone of my life of prayer; a constant reminder to renew my commitment to the Lord through conversion and charity.

⬛ Though often described as the Prayer of St Ignatius Loyola (1491–1556), the founder of the Jesuit Order of Priests and Brothers, it seems unlikely Ignatius wrote it.
   This passage was also chosen by Father Ross Jones SJ (see his entry on page 102), who makes this observation:

FATHER ROSS JONES SJ
Often called the 'Prayer for Generosity', this petition expresses a desire for large-heartedness and service of others. As such it embraces so many images and stories of the 'Good News': love of neighbour, the good samaritan, the last judgement (the sheep and goats story in Matthew), to name but a few. And, of course, it is a disposition 'the Lord deserves' precisely because it describes Jesus' own disposition entirely. 'The man for others', as Dietrich Bonhoeffer described Jesus. The prayer is loved by young people because it taps into their natural idealism.

TIM WINTON

An acclaimed Australian author, Tim has written twenty books, won numerous literary awards and twice been shortlisted for the Booker Prize. His books have been published in more than eighteen languages and have been adapted for stage, film and radio. Tim is also an environmental activist.

You know ... when daylight starts, it wakes me up. I can't sleep any more. It wakes the whole body. So I turn round to have a look. There is brightness. Piccaninny daylight makes you feel like a different person. Morning gives you the flow of a new day – aah! With this beautiful colour inside, the sun is coming up, with that glow that comes straight away in the morning. The colour comes towards me and the day is waiting. You have a feeling in your heart that you're going to feed your body this day, get more knowledge. You go out now, see animals moving, see trees, a river. You are looking at nature and giving it your full attention, seeing all its beauty. Your vision has opened and you start learning now.

When you touch them, all things talk to you, give you their story. It makes you really surprised. You feel you want to get deeper, so you start moving around and stamp your feet – to come closer and to recognise what you are seeing. You understand that your mind has been opened to all those things because you are seeing them; because your presence and their presence meet together and you recognise each other. These things recognise you. They give you wisdom and their understanding to you when you come close to them.

In the distance you feel: 'Aaahh – I am going to go there and have a closer look!' You know it is pulling you. When you recognise it, it gives strength – a new flow. You have life now.

David Mowaljarlai

Reflections

Most of the unheeded and deep-rooted wisdom in Australia is Aboriginal, but it's so rarely given its due and the broader culture is impoverished as a result. Mowaljarlai was probably one of the most impressive Australians of the twentieth century, one of our few true visionaries. This is about addressing what most of us are worst at – paying attention.

● Excerpt from David Mowaljarlai and Jutta Malnic, *Yorro Yorro*, Inner Traditions International and Magabala Books, Broome, 1993.

David Mowaljarlai (c.1928–177) was a Ngarinyin elder, lawman and an early member of both the Aboriginal Arts Board of the Australia Council and the Australian Institute of Aboriginal and Torres Strait Islander Studies. He was Aboriginal of the Year in 1991.

CLINICAL PROFESSOR
FIONA WOOD, FRANCS AM

Fiona is dedicated to research and education into burns, trauma and scarless healing. She is co-founder of Clinical Cell Culture and chairman of the McComb Research Foundation. Her work with victims of the Bali bombings brought her to national prominence. Fiona was Australian of the Year in 2005.

> This is the true joy in life, the being used for a purpose recognised by yourself as a mighty one; the being a force of nature instead of a feverish, selfish little clod of ailments and grievances complaining that the world will not devote itself to making you happy.
>
> I am of the opinion that my life belongs to the whole community, and as long as I live it is my privilege to do for it whatever I can.
>
> I want to be thoroughly used up when I die, for the harder I work the more I live. I rejoice in life for its own sake. Life is no 'brief candle' for me. It is a sort of splendid torch which I have got hold of for the moment, and I want to make it burn as brightly as possible before handing it on to future generations.
>
> Attributed to George Bernard Shaw

Reflections

This passage was given to me at a time of intense work and achievement, by a nurse, Sheila, with whom I have worked with for many years.

● Excerpt from George Bernard Shaw, 'A Splendid Torch'.
George Bernard Shaw (1856–1950) was an Irish dramatist, critic and novelist. While Shaw was certainly the author of part of this passage (extracted from his preface to 'A speech at Brighton') the remainder has not been verified in a text.

GLOSSARY

AD – *Anno Domini* indicates the number of years that have passed since the birth of Christ.

AH – *Anno Hegirae* – the starting point of the Muslim calendar; the flight of the Prophet Muhammad from Mecca to Medina 622 AD.

BC – Before Christ – indicating years numbered back from the year of the birth of Christ.

Caliph – the title of the successors of Muhammad as leaders of the Islamic world, later assumed by the Sultans of Turkey.

CE – Common Era – period beginning with year of Christ's birth.

DD – Doctor of Divinity.

Hadith – recorded sayings and deeds of the Prophet Muhammad.

Imam – a religious leader, or an Islamic community leader or scholar.

JLC – Licentiate of Canon Law.

OP – Order of Preachers (official title of the Dominican Order).

Pantheism – Pantheists derive their fundamental religious experience through a personal relationship with the universe. They feel that nature is the ultimate context for human existence and seek to improve their relationship with the natural world as their fundamental religious responsibility.

Qur'an – the message from (God) Allah to humanity, transmitted over a period of twenty-three years (610 CE 622 CE) through the angel Gabriel to the Prophet Muhammad. The language of the original message is Arabic, which has been translated into many other languages.

In *Mosaic*, quoted sections or 'surahs' from the Holy Qur'an are from two translations: *The Meaning of the Glorious Qur'an*, published in 1930 by Muhammad Marmaduke Pickthall, or *The Holy Qur'an: Text, Translation and Commentary*, published in 1934 by Abdullah Yusuf Ali.

Sages – according to Hinduism, Sages are those who have renounced worldly life and attained a high stage in spiritual life, enabling them to give advice about religious rituals and worship.

SDB– an international organisation of Catholic priests and brothers dedicated to the service of the young, especially the disadvantaged.

Siddur – daily prayers are collected in a book called a 'siddur', which derives from the Hebrew root meaning 'order', because the siddur shows the order of prayers. It is the same root as the word 'seder', which refers to the Passover home service.

SJ– Society of Jesus

SM– Society of Mary

Yiddish – a language spoken as a vernacular by Jews in Europe and elsewhere by Jewish emigrants, usually written in the Jewish alphabet. Historically, it is a dialect of High German with an admixture of words of Hebrew, Romance, and Slavonic origin, developed in central and eastern Europe during the Middle Ages.

Vedas – written in Sanskrit, contain religious hymns and rituals which are used in worship and in day-to-day life. These are among the most ancient religious texts still in existence. Enunciated by Sages in ancient times, they take pride of place in the Hindu religion, embodying many mantras and powerful prayers.

ACKNOWLEDGEMENTS

Many people have assisted in *Mosaic* becoming a reality and I would like to sincerely thank them for their encouragement, interest and wisdom. Primarily, I would like to express my appreciation to all those who contributed to *Mosaic*. Their inspiring insights enabled me to capture this picture of contemporary Australian identity.

I am also grateful to Julie Crawford for her editorial skills, and candid, considered thinking in shaping *Mosaic* before it went to the publisher; Rhonda Prentice who helped write and research some of the biographies; my twin brother Martin Manser for sharing his valuable editorial experience; Christobel Wescombe who taught me the true value of libraries; Bryony Gammon for her thoughtful comments; Julie, Owen, Nikki and Jenna Tregarthen for their enthusiasm and contacts; Sally Charkos and Caroline Lawrence for their encouragement and assistance during some difficult weeks; Father Herman Roborgh, Jesuit priest and Islamic scholar, for his insightful comments on the Islamic contributions; Frances Rush for her constructive thinking and Alice Svendsen who brought calm and order to my office.

Some contributors were particularly helpful including Professor Jennie Brand-Miller and Clive Norton who both offered insightful advice; Aziza Abdel-Halim; Mehmet Ozalp, Zuleyha Keskin, Mahsheed Ansari from Affinity Intercultural Foundation; Avril Alba and Rabbis Zalman Kastel and Jacki Ninio for their time and assistance; Larissa Behrendt, Father Frank Brennan, Dr Mary Crock, Cath DeVyre, Joe El-Khoury, Dani Haski, Melanie Hogan, Gabi Hollows, Silma Ihram, Jane Jeffes, Professor Gerald O'Collins, Ron Natoli, Carol Palmer, Beverley Polzin and Bob Randall.

Others who offered advice or assistance include: Francine Cavanagh, Yvonne Chandler, Vivienne Correa, June Dallas, Trevor Dalziell, Dr Garry Darby, Tamara Domicelj, Janette Doolan, Jacqui Field, Ernie Friedlander, Shane Garland, Liz Gill, Alan Hamilton, Peta Kearney, Helen Hill, Cath Lavelle, the Loxton family, Liz McCarthy, Colleen Orr, Jacinta Stephan, Sudhan Sundaram, Jill Taylor, the Rev'd David Thomas and Cecille Weldon. The following organisations were generous with their help: the Australian Society of Authors, the Women's Interfaith Network and the Jessie Street National Women's Library. Margaret Gee's *Australian Celebrity Contact Book* was invaluable.

The spirit of generosity with which so many copyright-holders responded to requests was affirming, and to them I offer my deep appreciation.

Thanks also to Helen Littleton at ABC Books, for her faith in the concept of *Mosaic* and for her encouragement along its journey, and to Anne Reilly, for her attention to detail in chasing up the permissions and copyright, despite the many hurdles, and for her editorial expertise.

My family put up with my long hours on the computer and relayed phone messages from *Mosaic* contacts. They offered encouragement during the hectic days and loud exclamations when I received a wonderful contribution. My gratitude and heartfelt thanks to Steve, Sam, Jess and Nick.

A NOTE ON SOURCES

Every effort has been made to attribute and trace the original source and/or current copyright holder for the poems or reflections that appear in this collection. Where these attempts have been unsuccessful, the author and publisher would be pleased to hear from the copyright holders to rectify any omission in future reprints of this book. All attributions appear with the contribution. Additionally we are grateful for permission to reprint the following copyright material:

INDEX OF CONTRIBUTORS

A

Abdalla, Mohamad 1
Abdel-Fattah, Randa 2
Abdel-Halim, Aziza 3
Alba, Avril 4
Alhadeff, Vic 5
Ali, Ameer 6–7
Ansari, Mahsheed 8–9
Aspinall, Phillip 10
Atem, Adut Dau 11

B

Babbage, Stuart Barton 12
Baber, Margot 13–14
Baliozian, Aghan 15–16
Behrendt, Larissa 16
Bell, John 17
Birch, Charles 18
Brady, Veronica 19
Brahm, Ajahn 20–21
Brand-Miller, Jennie 22
Brennan, Frank 23
Broadbridge, Trisha 24
Bryant, Lucinda 25
Buchanan, Andrew 26–27
Burney, Linda 27–28
Burnside, Julian 29

C

Caldicott, Helen 30
Carroll, Peter 31
Carroll, Tamsin 32–33
Cassidy, Idris Edward 34–35
Celik, Fulya 35–36
Chamberlain-Creighton, Lindy 37
Chandab, Taghred 38

Clark, Graeme 39
Clifford, Kareena 40
Coleman, Paul 41
Corbett, Roger 42
Costello, Tim 43–44
Cowley, Camilla 45
Crews, Bill 46–47
Crock, Mary 48
Cuthbert, Betty 49

D

Darveniza, Paul 50
Dawe, Bruce 51
Deane, William 52
Denton, Andrew 53
Devrye, Catherine 54–55
Do, Khoa 56
Doherty, Peter 57–58
Done, Ken 58
Dowrick, Stephanie 59–60
Ducker, Heath 60
Dunphy, Dexter 61

E

Eales, John 62–63
El-Khoury, Joe 64–65
Ellis, Liz 66
Englebrecht, Kate 67
Eves, Hayley 68

F

Fawkner, Patty 69–70
Field, Anthony 70
Fischer, Tim 71–72
Fong, King 73
French, Jackie 74

G

Gallagher, Harry 75
Gill, Richard 76
Ginibi, Ruby Langford 77–78
Goode, Katherine 79–80
Guiton, Gerard 80–81

H

Harmer, Joyce 81–82
Haski, Dani 83–84
Henderson, Anne 85
Hinton, Phillip 86–87
Hogan, Melanie 87
Hollingworth, Peter 88
Hollows, Gabi 89
Holmes, Margaret 90

I

Ihram, Silma 91

J

Janke, Terri 92–93
Jeffes, Jane 93–94
Jeffries, Sam 95
Jones, Caroline 96
Jones, Ross 97

K

Kastel, Zalman 98–99
Kee, Jenny 100
Keskin, Zuleyha 101
Kiernan, Ian 102
King, Petrea 103
Kirby, Michael 104–5
Kremmer, Christopher 105

L

Leung, Lucilla 106
Lewis, Tom E 107–8
Lowy, Frank 109

M

Maclurcan, Don 110
Madigan, Trish 111
Malki Malki, Mor Malatius 112
Martin, Amanda 113
Martin, Jesse 114
Maulder, Jessie 115
McCallum, Ron 116–17
McMullen, Jeff 118
McPharlin, Luke 119
McRae-McMahon, Dorothy 120
Mehta, Mala 121–22
Mein, Jim 122–23
Melkonian, Harry 124
Menteith, Richard 125–26
Miller, Harry M 126–27
Munro, Mike 127
Murdoch, Elisabeth 128
Murray, Les 129

N

Natoli, Ron 130
Newcombe, John 131–32
Ninio, Jacqueline 133
Norton, Clive 134
Nossal, Gustav 135

O

O'Collins, Gerald 136
Olsen, John 137
O'Neill, Susie 138
Ozalp, Mehmet 139–40

P

Palmer, Carol 140–41
Pell, George 142
Pellach, Peta Jones 143
Phillips, Gregory 144
Pickhaver, Greig 145–46
Pieters-Hawke, Sue 146

Polzin, Beverley 147
Porter, Chester 148
Porter, Muriel 148

R
Randall, Bob 149–50
Rawi, Mahboba 151
Ridgeway, Aden 152–53
Riley, Chris 153
Robinson, Ian 154
Rose, Heather 155

S
Salehi, Nouria Sultana 156–57
Saliba, Paul 157
Sarra, Chris 158
Sculthorpe, Peter 159
Seen, Frances 160
Seyit, Kuranda Seyfettin 161
Shatford, Ruth 162
Sherman, Gene 163
Singer, Peter 164
Singh, Moninder 165
Sinn, Steve 166

Slater, Keith 167
So, John 168
Solomon, Charmaine 169–70
Steer, Naomi 171
Strong, James 172
Stylianos, Archbishop 173
Sundaram, Sinna 174

T
Tedeschi, Simon 175–76
Tingwell, Charles 'Bud' 176
Tooth, John 177–78
Trad, Keysar 179

U
Uren, Tom 180–81

V
Van Der Linden, Sabina 183–84
Vanas, Adrian 182–83

W
Walton, Nancy Bird 184
Warren, Guy 185

INDEX OF SOURCES

A

al–Kabir, Al–Jawshan, 35–36
al–Khattab, Umar bin, 1
Ali, Abdullah Yusuf, 3
Allen, James, 158
Amnon, Rabbi, 109
Anonymous or unattributed, 12, 53,
  56, 60, 75, 124, 138, 153, 160,
  177–78
Ansari, Sheikh, 151
Armstrong, Karen, 120
Atem, Adut Dau, 171
Author unknown, *see* Anonymous
  or unattributed

B

Bahá'u'lláh, 119
Bernard of Clairvaux, Saint, 142
Bible
  Colossians 3:12–15:, 31
  Deuteronomy 32:10–12:, 41
  Ecclesiastes 3:1–8:, 128
  Habakkuk 3:17–19:, 85
  I Corinthians 4:7:, 39
  I Corinthians 13:, 27–28
  Isaiah 40:31:, 49
  Isaiah 42:1–4:, 23
  Isaiah 58:6–7:, 45
  John 1:1–18:, 71–72
  John 3:16:, 42
  Lord's Prayer, 46–47
  Matthew 25:35–40:, 52
  Matthew 5: 6, 9–10:, 135
  Philippians 3:12–16:, 122–23
  Philippians 4:4–9:, 111
  Psalm 23:, 19
  Psalm 46:7:, 148
  Psalm 51:1–3:, 157
  Psalm 90:14:, 113
  Psalm 100:, 76
  Psalm 121:1–2,7–8:, 96
  Psalm 130:, 34–35
Blake, William, 175–76
Book of Common Prayer, 104–5
Brahm, Ajahn, 20–21
Brink, André, 93–94
Broadbridge, Trisha, 24

C

Caldicott, Helen, 30
Carnegie, Jon, 24
Chicago, Judy, 133
Conrad, Joseph, 114
Countryman, L William, 140–41
Cranmer, Archbishop Thomas,
  104–5
Crosby, Fanny, 81–82

D

Dalai Lama, 115
Dawe, Bruce, 51
de Gasztold, Carmen Bernos,
  183–84
Deveson, Anne, 26–27
DeVrye, Catherine, 54–55
Donne, John, 50
Duncan, Bonnie, 13–14

E

Eales, John, 62–63
Ehrmann, Max, 163
Eliot, TS, 66
Emerson, Ralph Waldo, 110

F

Fong, King, 73
Fox, George, 80–81
Francis of Assisi, Saint, 43–44, 103
French, Jackie, 74

G

Gandhi, Mahatma, vi
Gasztold, Carmen Bernos de,
    183–84
Ginibi, Ruby Langford, 77–78
Giocondo, Fra Giovanni, 188–89
Goethe, Johann Wolfgang von, 184
Golden Rule, 172
Griffin, Gerald, 70

H

Hail Mary, 127
Havel, Václav, 186–87
Heaney, Seamus, 67
Hillel, Rabbi, 4
Hopkins, Gerard Manley, 137
Hunter, Robert, 145–46

J

Jackson, Jill, 68
Janke, Toni, 92–93
Janki, Dadi, 126–27
Jeffries, Sam, 95
Jewish Prayer, 59–60, 79–80
John of Sedreh, Saint, 112
John XXII, Pope, 166

K

Kabir, Al-Jawshan al-, 35–36
Kastel, Rabbi Zalman, 98–99
Khan, Hazrat Inayat, 59–60
Khattab, Umar bin al-, 1
King, Martin Luther Jr, 16

Kipling, Rudyard, 131–32
Lakota Prayer, 155
Lawrence, DH, 116–17
Leung, Lucilla, 106
Leunig, Michael, 10, 22
Lewis, Tom E, 107–8
Lord's Prayer, 46–47
Loyola, St Ignatius, 97, 193

M

MacLean, Alistair, 162
Mantra, Gayathri, 174
Markova, Dawna, 152–53
McMullen, Jeff, 25, 118
Merton, Thomas, 154, 190
Mowaljarlai, David, 194–95
Muhammad, 38, 101, 139–40
Murray, Les, 129

N

Nanak, Guru, 165
Natoli, Ron, 130
Newman, John Henry, 88
Niebuhr, Reinhold, 146
Nursi, Bediuzzaman Said, 8–9

P

Pellach, Peta Jones, 143
Penn, William, 147
Pound, Ezra, 57–58
Powers, Jessica, 69–70

Q

Qur'an
    v 1:1-7:, 156–57
    v 49:13:, 2
    v 87:1–10:, 91
    v 112:1–4:, 191

R

Rado, James, 32–33
Ragni, Gerome, 32–33
Randall, Bob, 149–50
Rice, Helen Steiner, 125–26
Richard of Chichester, Saint, 136
Rose, Danielle, 64–65
Rosh Hashanah Meditation, 83–84
Rumi, Mawlana Jalalud'din, 161
Rupp, Joyce, 40
Rutter, John, 48

S

Saint Martin de Porres Prayer, 89
Sanskrit proverb, 58
Sculthorpe, Peter, 159
Shakespeare, William, 17
Shaw, George Bernard, 102, 196
Shnorhali, Nerses, 15–16
Shutz, Brother Roger, 192
So, John, 168
Solomon, Charmaine, 169–70
Spender, Stephen, 86–87
Spira, Henry, 164
Stuart, Muriel, 90
Stylianos, Archbishop, 173
Syed, Ameer Ali, 6–7

T

Tagore, Rabindranath, 105, 121–22
Third Order, Society of St Francis, 167
Thomas the Contender, 61
Thurber, James, 29
Tibetan mantra, 100
Tingwell, Bud, 176
Trad, Keysar, 179

U

Unattributed, *see* Anonymous or unattributed
Uren, Tom, 180–81

V

Vanas, Adrian, 182–83
von Goethe, Johann Wolfgang, 184

W

Warren, Guy, 185
Watson, Aunty Lilla, 144
Whitehead, Alfred North, 18
Whittier, John Greenleaf, 37
Wilhelmsson, Märta, 148

ABOUT THE AUTHOR

Rosalind Bradley was born and raised in the UK and has lived in Australia for the last 23 years. After working for two years in Papua New Guinea as a volunteer teacher, she later returned to live in Australia. She has worked in PR and marketing for several charities including The Fred Hollows Foundation.

Ros has an eclectic spiritual background including a Jewish heritage, agnostic upbringing, baptised and confirmed Anglican in her late twenties, worked in 'world development' for the Methodist Church, London and was received into the Catholic Church in Sydney 2002. She now lives in Sydney with her husband and three children.